The Sutra of Ksitigarbha's Fundamental Vows

A Colloquial Translation

A Vernacular Rendition
by Master Sheng Chang Hwang

Translated From the
Chinese Sūtra of Śikṣānanda

SOCIETY OF KSITIGARBHA STUDIES

In grateful memory of our mentor

Sheng Chang Hwang

A faithful disciple and good messenger of

Kṣitigarbha Bodhisattva

and

The Three Jewels

For his inexhaustible teachings and caring

The Sutra of Ksitigarbha's Fundamental Vows:
A Colloquial Translation

A Vernacular Rendition by Master Sheng Chang Hwang
Translated From the Chinese Sūtra of Śikṣānanda

© 2022 Society of Ksitigarbha Studies, USA

Revised Edition, December 2022.
Previous editions were published in 2017 and 2018 under different ISBNs.

Typeset in EB Garamond, 12.5pt.

BISAC Codes:
REL007030   RELIGION / Buddhism / Sacred Writings
REL007000   RELIGION / Buddhism / General
PHI028000   PHILOSOPHY / Buddhist

Paperback: ISBN 979-8-218-12688-9

Available from online stores such as Amazon as well as bookstores and
libraries via IngramSpark.

USA:
Society of Ksitigarbha Studies, USA
Dong Shan Institute of Buddhism
23811 122nd Ave. East
Graham, WA 98338, USA
Tel: +1 (360) 893-8814
usa@ksitigarbha-studies.org / info@dongshaninstitute.org

HONG KONG:
Society of Ksitigarbha Studies Foundation, Hong Kong, Limited
hk@ksitigarbha-studies.org

TAIWAN:
Society of Ksitigarbha Studies, Taiwan
taiwan@ksitigarbha-studies.org

www.ksitigarbha-studies.org

Table of Contents

Preface
Revised 2022 Edition

We would like to express our gratitude to Ms. Alice Grundböck of Austria for reaching out to us as this revised edition would not have been compiled so soon without the interest of her and the group she was representing. It gave us the chance to review the first edition and make some important, necessary improvements for which we are grateful.

We are also indebted to many people and their resources in helping to improve the Buddhist terms and Sanskrit meanings including: *Wisdom Library* by Gabe Hiemstra, *Pleco* by Michael Love, Venerable Professor K.L. Dhammajoti, Dr. Dhammarakkhit, Dr. Gao Mingyuan, Professor Tony K. Lin, the Fo Guang Shan International Translation Center and *Chinese & Japanese Online Dictionary* by Oriental Outpost.

In this revised edition, most updates are in the Endnotes and Glossary with added descriptions of the Buddhist terms, including more information about the Sanskrit (Skt.) words. A few changes in the sūtra were intended to reflect closer to the Chinese version so that the dharma can be better received.

In this chaotic, confusing and distressed world filled with greed, arrogance and contention, suffering is heightened leading to never-ending wars, pandemics and famine. Our hope is that these updates could be of help to the reader to understand and correspond with the sūtra more profoundly, be inspired by the kindness and mercy of the intricate, magnificent dharma and be even closer with the Three Jewels and Kṣitigarbha Bodhisattva Mahāsattva in order to find true salvation, liberation and happiness within.

Translation Team
DECEMBER 2022

Preface

Ever since late 1998, under the merciful blessing of the Buddha, Kṣitigarbha Bodhisattva Mahāsattva and the leadership of the late Master Sheng Chang Hwang, we—the practitioners and fellow students of Dong Shan Institute of Buddhism and the Society of Kṣitigarbha Studies—have been making a close connection with Kṣitigarbha Bodhisattva through earnest study of *The Sūtra of Kṣitigarbha's Fundamental Vows*. We have also been studying *The Sūtra of the Mahāyāna Great Assembly of Kṣitigarbha's Ten Wheels* and *The Sūtra of Divining and Examining the Retributions of Virtuous and Evil Deeds** and we pay daily tributes accordingly.

Since 2000, our bond with Kṣitigarbha has grown stronger because of repeated, miraculous and first-hand experiences of being rescued, a small part of which are documented in our newsletters. To reciprocate the grace of the Buddha, Kṣitigarbha and all sentient beings, as well as to make our lives meaningful and worthwhile, we have set our mission: to make it possible for all sentient beings to hear Kṣitigarbha's name, see His image, learn about His merits and know how to seek His rescue and be rescued.

To facilitate the growing number of English-speaking Buddhists to learn about Kṣitigarbha Bodhisattva who has been deputized by the Buddha to oversee the well-being of all sentient beings of this time and on this earth, a new translation of *The Sūtra of Kṣitigarbha's Fundamental Vows* was deemed necessary. After over eight years of team efforts, the preliminary work is completed, and the text has been test-studied by many old and new colleagues of ours with good, heart-warming responses. We pray that you, our readers, will find this Sūtra understandable and helpful in learning

---

*In Buddhism, the definition of *virtuous* is "beneficial with no harm" and the definition of *evil* is "harmful without benefit". There are ten evil deeds. What are virtuous deeds? Departing from the ten evil deeds is doing and practicing virtuous deeds. See *Ten Virtuous Disciplines* in Glossary.

The Sutra of Ksitigarbha's Fundamental Vows

about ourselves, our lives, our destinies, our world and this cosmic universe we are in.

All Buddhist sūtras were first recorded in one of the most ancient Indian languages—Sanskrit. In this translation we have kept many of the Buddhas' and Bodhisattvas' names, as well as many Buddhist terms, in Sanskrit with English spellings, which is only a regrettable compromise as we know very little about this sophisticated and precise language. We ask our readers' forgiveness if errors are present. Perhaps in the future, we can solicit some experts to help us present the Sanskrit alphabet correctly. During the translation we have used the Chinese and Sanskrit dictionaries compiled by Prof. Tony K. Lin and Josephine Lin as a reference.

This Sūtra translation is based on the Chinese text which was translated from Sanskrit by the great sūtra translator Śikṣānanda of Khotan in the 7th century. Even though the Chinese wordings are literally understandable, their profound meanings are yet to be explored and comprehended by each individual reader.

During our translation, great emphasis was placed to make the Sūtra meaningful. Thus, certain explicit explanations based upon Master Hwang's published teachings on this Sūtra have been added, mostly in brackets, to indicate such amendments. Subheadings in each chapter—added by the translators for easier learning—are also placed within brackets. Nevertheless, the best way to learn the Sūtra is to make the teachings relevant within our personal lives as well as the lives of other beings and also by teaming with a well-learned Buddhist mentor for guidance.

We have used *italics* to indicate two important properties of the text: (1) to indicate a Sanskrit word or a Buddhist terminology when it first appears in the text; and (2) to stress the importance of the Dharma-Doors-to-Enlightenment which are key practices that readers can make good use of in order to attain specific benefits and accelerate on the cultivation path.

Although some of the practices may initially appear too plain to be taken seriously, they are indeed powerful, intricate and effective when we follow the instructions closely. Our trust and faith can only be established through personal practice and validation. So we encourage our readers to give themselves a chance to harvest the effectiveness of the practices and to give Kṣitigarbha Bodhisattva a chance to prove that He is truly merciful, real and omnipresent.

For the convenience of reading and chanting the Sūtra in unison, we have placed endnotes in the back of the book. A ten-point Study Guide from Master Hwang allows the reader to delve deeper into the meaning of the Sūtra.

Three prayers—*Prayer before Reading The Sūtra of Kṣitigarbha's Fundamental Vows, Prayer for the Dying and Newly Deceased* and *My Pledge*—written by Master Hwang are also included. The first prayer is for reading this particular Sūtra. Names of the sick, newborn babies or those in need of blessings can be added in the blanks. A second prayer is for the dying and newly deceased, which is to be read for the terminally ill and within 49 days from the day of a person's death. The third prayer, *My Pledge*, is for those who want to generate the greatest benefits from studying this Sūtra. To enhance our vows and to seek higher guidance, read *The Four Grand Vows* and *Opening Prayer before Reading a Sūtra* before or after reading the first prayer or all prayers.

In viewing the completion of this translation, our team wishes to extend our deepest gratitude to Śākyamuni Buddha, Kṣitigarbha Bodhisattva Mahāsattva and Master Sheng Chang Hwang, who passed away in June 2009. Also, our gratitude goes to our first copy-editor Michael Alperstein.

May our readers find this Sūtra enlightening and beneficial, and may it inspire a journey of truthful homage and emancipation. We would be happy to hear from you if we can be of further assistance.

Translation Team
JUNE 2017

The Sutra of Ksitigarbha's Fundamental Vows

The Four Grand Vows

Sentient beings are infinite, I vow to transform them all;

Troubles are endless, I vow to cease them all;

Dharma conveniences are countless, I vow to learn them all;

The Buddha's Path is unsurpassed, I vow to realize it all.

❧

Opening Prayer before Reading a Sūtra

This unsurpassed, profound, intricate and wondrous dharma

is hard to encounter in hundreds of thousands of millions of kalpas.

Now I have the chance to see, hear, receive and uphold it,

I vow to unlock the true meaning of Tathāgata.

Prayer before Reading
The Sūtra of Kṣitigarbha's Fundamental Vows

With utmost sincerity, I contemplate the following thoughts:

I solely vow that when I open *The Sūtra of Kṣitigarbha's Fundamental Vows*, it will be as if I am personally attending the assembly in Trāyastriṃśa Heaven, listening to the teachings of Śākyamuni Buddha, Kṣitigarbha Bodhisattva Mahāsattva and many other Bodhisattva Mahāsattvas!

I vow: As I read this Sūtra, it will be as if the Buddha, the Bodhisattvas, God of Solid-Firm-Earth, Deva Yamarāja and many ghost kings are directly addressing the dharma to me.

I vow: I will be in full accordance with the dharma taught by those virtuous mentors wholeheartedly, vigilantly and profoundly.

I vow: I will often read and study this Sūtra with faith, appreciation, respect and mindfulness; I will contemplate the meaning without forgetting it; I will guard the dharma from extinction; and I will extensively spread the dharma to all beings in the future so that they will also gain the benefits.

I vow: By relying on the merits gained from reading and studying this Sūtra, I will attain a firm dharma connection with Kṣitigarbha Bodhisattva Mahāsattva.

I vow: I will attribute the merits gained from reading and studying this Sūtra to the wisdom and consciousness that have long been hidden and to Anuttara-samyak-saṃbodhi.

I vow: I will attribute the merits gained from reading and studying this Sūtra to the Path of Ten Virtuous Deeds.

I vow: I will attribute the merits gained from reading and studying this Sūtra to all sinful, suffering beings, as well as those in the six realms [of existence] and the ten directions [in this universe so that they will gain the same benefits].

I vow: I will attribute the merits gained from reading and studying this Sūtra to my past countless numbers of births and deaths—I vow that all beings and I can swiftly apply the merits of this Sūtra to find annulment of all sins accumulated from past infinite kalpas as a result of committing the Ten Evil Deeds, the Four Prohibitions, the Five Rebellious Sins, turning the truth upside down, slandering the Three Jewels and the deeds of Icchantika.

I vow: By relying on the merits gained from reading and studying this Sūtra, I will attribute all the merits to
_______*(insert names of those in concern)*_____ so that
_______*(insert names)*________________ will rely upon the meritorious power of this Sūtra to swiftly eliminate all evil deeds and grave sins, to part from all obstacles, all sufferings and hardships, and to swiftly gain blissful peace and refuge.

I vow: that _______*(insert names)*______________, all beings and I will soon have Kṣitigarbha Bodhisattva Mahāsattva's kind and merciful attention and nurturing, uplifting salvation and illuminating teaching and guidance.

Prayer for the
Dying and Newly Deceased

We bow deeply before the feet of Kṣitigarbha Bodhisattva Mahāsattva!

We respectfully make offerings and pay homage to Kṣitigarbha Bodhisattva Mahāsattva!

We take refuge in Kṣitigarbha Bodhisattva Mahāsattva!

We pray that Kṣitigarbha Bodhisattva Mahāsattva will swiftly and urgently rescue ____*(insert names of those in concern)*____ and all newly deceased beings.

We pray that Kṣitigarbha Bodhisattva Mahāsattva will strengthen us with kindness and mercy, deliverance and fearless-miraculous power as we make a vow to study *The Sūtra of Kṣitigarbha's Fundamental Vows* for the sake of delivering ____*(insert names)*____ and all newly deceased beings from great suffering and distress!

We pray that Kṣitigarbha Bodhisattva Mahāsattva will strengthen ____*(insert names)*____ and all newly deceased beings with kindness and mercy, deliverance and fearless-miraculous power, so that they can be blessed with bravery and honesty to confront all the ten evil deeds of action, speech and thought that they have committed. The evil deeds are:

> killing, stealing, sexual misconduct;
> deceptive speech, alienating speech, ill-intended speech, frivolous speech;
> greed/stinginess, hatred/jealousy and arrogance with erroneous views.

Empower them to repent for their sinful deeds so as to cleanse the evil karma and remove all obstacles as they travel onto a new path.

We pray that Kṣitigarbha Bodhisattva Mahāsattva will strengthen ______*(insert names)*______ and all newly deceased beings with kindness and mercy, deliverance, fearlessness and miraculous power, so they will have peaceful, benevolent and tender hearts that will enable them to forgive all their foes, forego all their grievances and consequently cleanse their evil karma and remove all obstacles.

We pray that Kṣitigarbha Bodhisattva Mahāsattva will enlighten ______*(insert names)*______ and all newly deceased beings, rescue ______*(insert names)*______ and all newly deceased beings, lead ______*(insert names)*______ and all newly deceased beings and spare them from great sufferings. Spare them from falling into the three evil realms of hell, animals and hungry ghosts. Guide them to be reborn in a blissful place among human or celestial beings. Allow them to follow Kṣitigarbha Bodhisattva closely, life after life.

Namaḥ Kṣitigarbhāya Bodhisattvāya Mahāsattvāya!*
Namaḥ Kṣitigarbhāya Bodhisattvāya Mahāsattvāya!
Namaḥ Kṣitigarbhāya Bodhisattvāya Mahāsattvāya!

**Namaḥ* is a Sanskrit word for "homage".
Namaḥ Kṣitigarbhāya means "homage to Kṣitigarbha".

My Pledge

As a disciple of the Three Jewels, I _______ *(your name)* _______, in front of the image of Kṣitigarbha Bodhisattva Mahāsattva and with utmost sincerity and respect, make the following grand vows:

Namaḥ Kṣitigarbhāya Bodhisattvāya Mahāsattvāya!
Namaḥ Kṣitigarbhāya Bodhisattvāya Mahāsattvāya!
Namaḥ Kṣitigarbhāya Bodhisattvāya Mahāsattvāya!

I vow: that all sentient beings and I will often receive, uphold, study and chant *The Sūtra of Kṣitigarbha's Fundamental Vows*;

I vow: that while receiving, upholding, studying and chanting this Sūtra, I will profoundly comprehend the true, dependable meaning of the Buddha and Bodhisattvas;

I vow: to protect and uphold this Sūtra and Kṣitigarbha's convenient practices until all sinful-suffering beings on this earth are transformed and liberated;

I vow: that all my parents, spouses, brothers, sisters, sons, daughters, other dependents of my numerous past lives as well as all sinful-suffering beings on this earth will rely on the merits of this Sūtra to be rescued and transformed;

I vow: that in all the Buddha lands where there are hells, all sinful-suffering beings will rely on the merits of this Sūtra to be rescued and transformed;

I vow: that at all times and at all places, all sentient beings will make the same pledge as I so that we can be empowered by the miraculous power of Kṣitigarbha Bodhisattva's grand vow to gain the benefits of:

> Departing from the Five Unremitting Hells,
> from all large and small hells,
> from the three evil realms,
> from reincarnations amongst the six realms,
> from the Burning Three Realms,
> from the suffering sea of births and deaths;
>
> Forever departing from all Eight Sufferings; and
>
> Relying on the Authentic Teachings and Conveniences
> of Tathāgata to reach the Buddha's realm together,
> to validate the Buddha's stage together, and
> to enjoy the grand nirvāṇa of true permanence, true happiness,
> true identity ("I") and true cleanliness together;

I vow: to follow Kṣitigarbha Bodhisattva to transform all sinful-suffering beings on this earth until Maitreya Bodhisattva becomes a Buddha;

I vow: with this pledge, to draw and receive the empowerment of Kṣitigarbha Bodhisattva's miraculous power generated from this grand vow upon me;

I vow: by relying upon the miraculous power of Kṣitigarbha's grand vow, to completely and satisfactorily accomplish my pledge;

I vow: that with the merits from my pledge, I make:

> Respectful offerings to all the Buddhas in the
> past, present and future,
>
> Respectful offerings to the Three Jewels, and
>
> Respectful offerings to Kṣitigarbha Bodhisattva
> Mahāsattva;

I vow: that I will attribute the merits of my pledge to all sentient beings of the past, present and future in the ten dharma realms.

> *Namaḥ Kṣitigarbhāya Bodhisattvāya Mahāsattvāya!*
> *Namaḥ Kṣitigarbhāya Bodhisattvāya Mahāsattvāya!*
> *Namaḥ Kṣitigarbhāya Bodhisattvāya Mahāsattvāya!*

The Sutra of Ksitigarbha's Fundamental Vows

CHAPTER 1:

Miracles in the Palace of Trāyastriṃśa Heaven

*[Subheadings in brackets added by the
translator for easier reading]*

The following *dharma*[1] is derived from my recollection of the teachings that I have heard in *Trāyastriṃśa Heaven*[2] where the *Buddha* expounded the dharma for His mundane mother *Lady Māyā*[3]. At that time, all the inexpressible-inexpressible[4] numbers of Buddhas and *Bodhisattva*[5] *Mahāsattvas*[6] came and assembled there from the infinite Buddha lands in the ten directions[7] of the universe.

Together they praised and hailed *Śākyamuni*[8] Buddha because He, in these evil times[9] with its Five Contaminations[10], is able to manifest inconceivable great wisdom and miraculous power to cultivate and tame obstinate, unyielding sentient beings[11] of this world that are hard-to-tame and transform. His teachings began with the *Law of Suffering and Happiness*[12]. Hence, representatives from all the Buddha lands were sent to pay respects to *Bhagavat*[13].

[Prelude]

At that time, *Tathāgata*[14] smiled and radiated hundreds of thousands of myriads of millions of majestic, illuminating clouds, namely:

> The majestic, illuminating clouds of perfection,
> The majestic, illuminating clouds of kindness and mercy,
> The majestic, illuminating clouds of wisdom,
> The majestic, illuminating clouds of *Prajñā*[15],
> The majestic, illuminating clouds of *Samādhi*[16],

The majestic, illuminating clouds of auspice,
The majestic, illuminating clouds of virtuous blessings,
The majestic, illuminating clouds of virtuous merits,
The majestic, illuminating clouds of homage[17], and
The majestic, illuminating clouds of praise and acclaim.

Having emitted these inexpressible numbers of illuminating clouds, He continued to give out various, infinite, exquisite voices, namely:

The voice of *Dāna*[18] *Pāramitā*[19],
The voice of *Śīla*[20] *Pāramitā*,
The voice of *Kṣānti*[21] *Pāramitā*,
The voice of *Vīrya*[22] *Pāramitā*,
The voice of *Dhyāna*[23] *Pāramitā*,
The voice of *Prajñā Pāramitā*,
The voice of Kindness and Mercy,
The voice of Rejoicing and Letting Go,
The voice of Deliverance,
The voice of No-Outflow *(an-āśrava)*[24],
The voice of Wisdom,
The voice of Great Wisdom,
The voice of Lion's Roar[25],
The voice of Great Lion's Roar,
The voice of Cloud Thunder, and
The voice of Great Cloud Thunder.

[*Assembly Attendants*]

After Śākyamuni Buddha sent out such inexpressible-inexpressible *dharma-voices*[26], infinite hundreds of millions of *devas*[27], *nāgas*[28], ghosts and gods from the *Sahā World*[29] and other worlds were inspired [and attracted by those illuminating *dharma-clouds*[30]

                    The Sutra of Kṣitigarbha's Fundamental Vows

and exquisite dharma-voices]. They came to attend this dharma assembly in *Trāyastriṃśa Palace*[31] from the following heavens[32]:

> Heaven of the Four Celestial Kings (*Catur-mahārāja-kāyika*),
> Trāyastriṃśa Heaven,
> Heaven of Virtue and Wonder (*Suyāma*),
> Heaven of Content and Knowledge (*Tuṣita*),
> Heaven of Joyful Transformations (*Nirmāṇa-rati*),
> Heaven of Mastery over Others' Transformations (*Para-nirmita-vaśavartin*),
> Heaven of the Multitudes of *Brahmā* (*Brahma-kāyika*),
> Heaven of the Ministers of Brahmā (*Brahma-purohita*),
> Heaven of the Great Brahmā (*Mahā-brahma*),
> Heaven of Lesser Light (*Parīttābha*),
> Heaven of Infinite Light (*Apramaṇabha*),
> Heaven of Light and Sound (*Ābhāsvara*),
> Heaven of Lesser Purity (*Parītta-śubha*),
> Heaven of Infinite Purity (*Apramāṇa-śubha*),
> Heaven of Universal Purity (*Śubha-kṛtsna*),
> Heaven of Blissful Birth (*Puṇya-prasava*),
> Heaven of Loving Blessings (*An-abhraka*),
> Heaven of Abundant Fruition (*Bṛhat-phala*),
> Heaven of No Thought (*Asaṃjñi-sattva*),
> Heaven of No Trouble (*Avṛha*),
> Heaven of No Heat (*Atapa*),
> Heaven of Virtuous Views (*Su-darśana*),
> Heaven of Virtuous Manifestations (*Su-dṛśa*),
> Ultimate Form Heaven (*A-kaniṣṭha*),
> Heaven of Infinite Space (*Ākāśānantyāyatana*),
> > [as well as a wide range of other heavens]
> > all the way through to
> Neither-Thinking-Nor-Not-Thinking Heaven
> > (*Naiva-saṃjñā-nāsaṃjñāyatana*).

All the devas, nāgas, ghosts, gods and others arrived and assembled there.

There were also many gods arriving from other worlds and the Sahā World, such as:

God of Oceans,
God of Rivers,
God of Creeks,
God of Trees,
God of Mountains,
God of Earth,
God of Streams and Lakes,
God of Crops,
God of Day,
God of Night,
God of Space,
God of Sky,
God of Food and Drink,
God of Grass and Vegetation, and
other such gods, all assembled there.

There were also many great ghost kings arriving from other worlds and the Sahā World, such as:

Evil-Eyed Ghost King,
Blood-Sucking Ghost King,
Spirit-Consuming Ghost King,
Ova-Devouring Ghost King,
Disease-Spreading Ghost King,
Poison-Commanding Ghost King,
Kind-Heart Ghost King,
Well-Being Ghost King,

  The Sutra of Ksitigarbha's Fundamental Vows

Great Love and Respect Ghost King, and
other such ghost kings, all assembled there.

[Introducing Kṣitigarbha Bodhisattva Mahāsattva]

At that time, Śākyamuni Buddha said to the Dharma Prince *Mañjuśrī*[33] Bodhisattva Mahāsattva: "Look at all the Buddhas, Bodhisattvas, devas, nāgas, ghosts and gods, from this Sahā World and other worlds, from this land and other lands, now assembled here in Trāyastriṃśa Heaven to attend this dharma gathering. Can you tell how many of them are here?"

Mañjuśrī replied to the Buddha: "O Bhagavat, even if I use my miraculous power for one thousand *kalpas*[34] of time to count the number, I could not tell how many are here."

The Buddha said to Mañjuśrī: "Even with the power of my Buddha-Eyes, I am not able to add up the number. These sentient beings are all related to *Kṣitigarbha*[35] Bodhisattva. From past infinite kalpas, some of them have been delivered and transformed[36]; some will be delivered and transformed during this assembly[37]; and some are yet to be delivered and transformed[38] in the future."

Mañjuśrī addressed the Buddha, saying: "Bhagavat! I have been cultivating virtuous roots[39] for a long time and have accomplished the Four Unhindered Wisdoms[40]; therefore, as soon as I hear your teaching, I am able to believe it, accept it, practice it and advocate it.

But for *śrāvakas*[41] seeking minor accomplishment [such as *Hīnayāna*[42] practitioners], the devas, nāgas and others of the Eight Legions[43], as well as sentient beings of future generations, although they hear your truthful words, they must still have doubts and confusion. Even if they are obliged to respectfully receive your words, inevitably they will slander the Three Jewels. Therefore, I wish wholeheartedly that you, Bhagavat, will talk extensively about what deeds[44] did Kṣitigarbha Bodhisattva Mahāsattva do during the cause-stages[45] and what vows He did make, so that He is able to accomplish such inconceivable tasks."

[The Vow's Time Span]

The Buddha said to Mañjuśrī: "For instance, if in the three thousandfold great cosmic worlds[46], we add each of all the grasses, shrubs, bushes, all the trees in the forests, all the rice, hemp, bamboo, reeds, all the rocks on the mountains and all the dust particles together, and consider each one as one Ganges River; then add all the grains of sand in all these Ganges Rivers together, and consider each grain as one realm[47]; within each realm, consider each dust particle as a kalpa; and then add all dust particles in one kalpa together as kalpas. The time span between now and when Kṣitigarbha Bodhisattva validated the Tenth Stage of the Bodhisattva's Path is one thousand times more than the time in the afore-mentioned metaphor, let alone the period when Kṣitigarbha Bodhisattva was a *Hearer*[48] and *Pratyeka-buddha*[49].

O Mañjuśrī, this Bodhisattva's grand vows have such inconceivable, majestic and miraculous power."

[Hearing His Name, Seeing His Image and Knowing His Merits]

"In the future, if there are virtuous men or women[50] who:

> *Hear the name of this Bodhisattva; and*
> *Begin to give praise and acclamation; or*
> *Gaze upon His image with admiration and obeisance; or*
> *Chant*[51] *His name and merits; or*

                    The Sutra of Kṣitigarbha's Fundamental Vows

Make offerings; or
Paint, sculpt or mold His image with colors,

They will be born in the Thirty-Three Heavens[52] for one hundred turns and will never again fall onto the evil paths[53] of existence."

[*The Vow of a Reputable Elder's Son—A Past Life of Kṣitigarbha*]

[The Buddha unfolded the following story:] "Mañjuśrī, this Kṣitigarbha Bodhisattva Mahāsattva, in the far remote past inexpressible-inexpressible kalpas ago, was once a son of a reputable elder. At that time, a Buddha was present in the world bearing the title *Lion Swift Vigorous All Deeds Well Accomplished Tathāgata*. When the elder's son saw the Buddha, with features so perfect and dazzling, symbolizing the immensity of His blessings and wisdom, he asked the Buddha, 'What deeds did you perform and what vow did you make so that you were able to acquire such great appearance and features?'

Then *Lion Swift Vigorous All Deeds Well Accomplished Tathāgata* replied to the elder's son, 'If you wish to realize such [good] appearance as I have, [you must make a vow that] for the infinite future, you must rescue and deliver all suffering sentient beings [as I have done].'

O Mañjuśrī, this was when the elder's son made his vow, saying, 'I vow—from now on until infinite future kalpas, I will prevalently use all kinds of convenient ways to rescue those sinful, suffering sentient beings in the six paths[54]. Only when they have reached ultimate liberation, will I realize the stage of a Buddha.'

Thus, he made this grand vow in front of that Buddha. From

that moment on, hundreds of thousands of myriads of millions of *nayuta*[55] kalpas have since passed, and he remains a Bodhisattva."

[The Vow of a Brahman Girl—Another Past Life of Kṣitigarbha]

"Moreover, in the past, inconceivable numbers of *asaṃkhyeya*[56] kalpas ago, a Buddha appeared in the world, bearing the name *Enlightenment Flower Samādhi Self-at-Ease King Tathāgata*, with a lifespan of four hundred quadrillion asaṃkhyeya kalpas. During the Dharma-Resemblance Period[57], there was a *brahman*[58] girl who possessed profound blissful merits due to the virtuous deeds[59] of her past lives. She was greatly admired, respected and guarded by many deities while she was walking, standing, sitting or sleeping.

Yet her mother took faith in the wrong ways and often slandered the Three Jewels. At that time, the brahman girl tried all kinds of convenient, prevalent ways to persuade her mother to have true faith and to adopt correct viewpoints; nevertheless, the mother did not fully accept the dharma. Soon afterwards, the mother passed away and reincarnated in Unremitting Hell[60].

The brahman girl knew that her mother did not believe the Law of Cause and Consequence[61] when she was alive. Thus, according to her karmic deeds, she would inevitably be reborn into the evil paths.

So the brahman girl sold her family possessions and made a generous and extensive search for all kinds of incense, flowers and other offerings to pay grand tribute to the past Buddha's *stūpas*[62] and temples [for the benefit of her mother].

She saw *Enlightenment Flower Samādhi Self-at-Ease King Tathāgata* whose image was in one of the temples, His sculpted

The Sutra of Kṣitigarbha's Fundamental Vows

statue most splendid, imposing and majestic. As the brahman girl gazed upon and reverently admired the image, she became more respectful and murmured to herself: 'The Buddha is the utmost enlightened being and possesses omniscient wisdom. If He were present in this world now, I could ask the Buddha the whereabouts of my mother after her death. He must know!'

At that time, the brahman girl was saddened and cried for quite a while. Then she looked up and gazed at Tathāgata's image with increasing admiration, desperately longing for His help.

Suddenly a voice spoke to her from mid-air, 'O weeping, saintly girl, don't be so sorrowful. I shall tell you the whereabouts of your mother.'

The brahman girl, facing mid-air with palms together, asked, 'Who is this deity that comforts my sadness and worry? Since I lost my mother, I cannot help but think of her day and night wondering where she is after her death, yet I have no place to make such an inquiry. Do you know where she has reincarnated?'

Then, the voice from mid-air responded to her again, 'I am the one you are gazing upon and paying homage to, the past *Enlightenment Flower Samādhi Self-at-Ease King Tathāgata*. Seeing that you mourn for your mother much more than other ordinary sentient beings would, I am here to tell you her whereabouts.'

Upon hearing these words, the brahman girl became frantic, jumped up and threw herself on the ground, gravely injuring her arms and legs. People next to her held her up, and it took quite a while before she regained consciousness. Once she did, she immediately turned to the mid-air and vowed, 'I wish that you, O

Buddha, would have kindness and mercy and tell me right away where my mother is reincarnated, because I am going to die soon [and I will go looking for her wherever she is reincarnated].'

At that time, *Enlightenment Flower Samādhi Self-at-Ease King Tathāgata* told the saintly girl, 'As soon as you finish making your offering, go back to your home, sit upright and contemplate my name and title with a focused mind. Then you will know the whereabouts of your mother.'

Then, the brahman girl immediately paid tribute to the Buddha and went home. In order to know her mother's whereabouts, she sat properly and contemplated the name and the merits of *Enlightenment Flower Samādhi Self-at-Ease King Tathāgata* with a focused mind.

After one day and one night, suddenly she found herself at the shore of a vast ocean, roaring and boiling. There were many wicked beasts with iron bodies. Some were flying over and some were running on the ocean, chasing their prey back and forth, vigorously trying to catch and devour the hundreds of thousands of millions of men and women floating and sinking in the waters.

She also saw many *yakṣas*[63] with different appearances—some with multiple arms, some with multiple eyes, some with multiple legs, and some with multiple heads, all of whom had teeth protruding from their mouths like sharp blades of a swift sword. The yakṣas drove the sinful people towards the wicked beasts [to be snatched, torn apart and devoured] and viciously fought with each other, their heads and limbs entwined together. Such horrible scenes varied in ten thousand different ways, and they would be hard for anyone to watch for long.

    The Sutra of Ksitigarbha's Fundamental Vows

At that time, the brahman girl was naturally not afraid because she had been empowered by contemplating [the name and the merits of] the Buddha.

Then, a Ghost King named *No-Poison* approached and saluted the saintly girl as a gesture of welcome, asking, 'Very Well! O Bodhisattva, why do you come here?'

The brahman girl asked the Ghost King, 'What is this place?'

No-Poison answered, 'This is the first ring of ocean west of the Great Iron-Enclosed Mountains (*Mahā-cakravāḍa*[64]).'

The saintly girl asked, 'I have heard that there are hells within the Great Iron-Enclosed Mountains. Is it true?'

No-Poison replied, 'Indeed there are!'

The saintly girl asked, 'How can I enter these Hells?'

No-Poison answered, 'Either by the majestic powers [of the Buddhas and Bodhisattvas] or by [heavy, evil] karmic forces. Without one or the other, no one can reach these hells.'

The saintly girl asked again, 'Why does this ocean boil and roil like this? And why are there so many sinful people and wicked beasts?'

No-Poison replied, 'These beings are the newly deceased from *Jambudvīpa*[65] who have committed evil deeds[66]. During and after the forty-nine day period [following their deaths], no one continued to perform any meritorious deeds on their behalf to save and deliver them from their sufferings[67]. Furthermore, when they were alive, they themselves did not perform any deeds as virtuous causes either. Therefore, based upon the evil deeds they have done, the karmic force of their deeds manifests the presence of these hells. [Driven by the force of their evil deeds] naturally they must pass this first ring of ocean.

However, to the east of this ocean, about one hundred thousand *yojanas*[68] away, there is another ring of ocean where the suffering is doubled. Further to the east, there is another ring of ocean to pass, and the suffering there is again multiplied.

[Why would these oceans appear here?] It is because the three evil deeds [of our action, speech and thought] manifest these oceans. These three rings of oceans are thus called the karmic seas.'

The saintly girl asked the Ghost King No-Poison again, 'Where are the Hells?'

No-Poison replied, 'Within these three rings of oceans, lie the great hells. There are hundreds of thousands of them, and each one is different. Within these great hells, there are eighteen major hells, which are then further subdivided into five hundred hells, where suffering and harm are infinite. These are then further subdivided into hundreds of thousands of hells, also with infinite suffering.'

The saintly girl asked the great Ghost King again, 'My mother died not long ago, and I wonder in which realm she is reincarnated?'

The Ghost King asked the saintly girl, 'When your mother was alive, what kinds of deeds did she do?'

The saintly girl answered, 'When my mother was alive, she often upheld erroneous views. She mocked and slandered the Three

   The Sutra of Ksitigarbha's Fundamental Vows

Jewels. At times she would accept correct views, but would soon become disrespectful again. Although she died recently, I have no idea where she has reincarnated.'

No-Poison asked, 'What was your mother's name?'

The saintly girl answered, 'Both my father and mother were brahmans. My father's name was Shi-luo-shan-xian, and my mother's name was Yue-di-li.'

No-Poison brought his palms together and said to the Bodhisattva, 'O Saintly One, please go back to where you came from [because you won't find your mother here], and you don't need to be so sad and worried when thinking of her. The sinful woman Yue-di-li [did come here to *Avīci Hell*[69], but she has left and] has been reincarnated in the celestial realm for three days. It was said that she was fortunate to have a filial[70] offspring like you who cultivated merits for her by [letting go of the family possessions and] making large offerings to pay tribute to the stūpas and temples of *Enlightenment Flower Samādhi Self-at-Ease King Tathāgata*.

Therefore, O Bodhisattva! Not only did your mother attain deliverance from hell, all sinful beings in Unremitting Hell [that were with her] on this day also reincarnated [in the celestial realm] together to enjoy blissful happiness.'

After the Ghost King finished his words, with palms together, he made an obeisance and withdrew.

The brahman girl came out of the meditation as if waking up from a dream and further contemplated the whole event. She made a grand vow in front of the statue of *Enlightenment Flower Samādhi Self-at-Ease King Tathāgata*, 'I vow, through infinite future kalpas, to rescue all sinful, suffering beings with all kinds of convenient *dharma-doors-to-enlightenment*[71] to help them gain deliverance.'"

The Buddha said to Mañjuśrī: "No-Poison Ghost King, then, is now Leading-Wealth Bodhisattva, and the brahman girl is now Kṣitigarbha Bodhisattva."

CHAPTER 2:

The Assembly of Divided-Identical Kṣitigarbha Bodhisattvas

[The Presence of Divided-Identical Kṣitigarbha Bodhisattvas]

At that time [in the ten directions of this universe], from hundreds of thousands of myriads of millions of unthinkable, indiscussable, immeasurable and unspeakable[72] infinite asaṃkhyeya worlds, wherever any of these worlds has a hell, the divided-identical (*vigraha*)[73] Kṣitigarbha Bodhisattvas [from those hells] all came and assembled in the palace of Trāyastriṃśa Heaven.

Inspired and moved by the miraculous power of Tathāgata, there were innumerable sentient beings—tens of thousands of millions upon millions of nayuta of them from all directions—who had been liberated from the path of karmic reincarnation in the six realms. Together, they came along with incense and flowers to make offerings to the Buddha. They had been taught and delivered by Kṣitigarbha Bodhisattva, and their determined minds, intent on seeking *Anuttara-samyak-saṃbodhi*[74], would never regress.

These sentient beings, from the remote, long kalpas of the past, had been wandering in the bitter sea of birth-and-death, stumbling and suffering in the six paths of reincarnation without a moment of rest. Relying on Kṣitigarbha Bodhisattva's immense kindness and mercy as well as profound vows, each of these sentient beings had validated various levels of sagehood[75]. Having arrived at Trāyastriṃśa Palace, they were exceedingly overjoyed. They gazed admiringly and respectfully at Tathāgata, their eyes not leaving Him for a moment.

[The Buddha's Entrustment]

At that time, Bhagavat extended His golden-bronze-colored arms to bless and touch the heads of all the divided-identical Kṣitigarbha Bodhisattva Mahāsattvas from hundreds of thousands of myriads of millions of unthinkable, indiscussable, immeasurable and unspeakable asaṃkhyeya worlds, saying:

"I have taught and transformed many obstinate, hard-to-tame beings in this foul time with the Five Contaminations, making their minds tame and virtuous. Among those who have forsaken all their devious and evil ways and taken homage in the true dharma and the right ways, there are one or two out of ten. For those who still have the habit to do evil, I have also transformed myself into tens of thousands of billions of entities [like you] and applied an infinite number of vast, convenient methods to rescue them.

There were those with sharp and wise roots[76]. As soon as they heard the dharma, they believed in and abided by it. There were those who had done many virtuous deeds with plenty of mundane blessings[77], but they needed to be inspired and encouraged from time to time to remember that favorable consequences are the result of doing virtuous deeds. There were those who were dim and dull that required long, continuous efforts to enlighten them before they would take homage in the Three Jewels. There were those who had serious evil karma who would not be respectful towards the Three Jewels.

Since these beings were under different karmic influences and capacities, it was necessary to appear in front of each of them as an equal, transformational entity[78] in order to rescue them. [To a man or a woman] I would transform myself into the form of a man or

 The Sutra of Kṣitigarbha's Fundamental Vows

a woman; or [to a deva] I would appear as a deva, and so on with nāgas, gods or ghosts. I would even manifest myself as a mountain, a forest, a river, a plain, a stream, a pond, a spring or a well. Using these convenient techniques, I would influence, inspire and rescue all these beings.

[Sometimes] I would transform myself into the form of a *devarāja*[79], a *brahmarāja*[80], a wheel-turning king[81], a lay Buddhist, a king, a minister or an officer; [sometimes as] a *bhikṣu* or a *bhikṣuṇī*[82], an *upāsaka* or an *upāsikā*[83], or even in the form of a śrāvaka, an *arhat*[84], a pratyeka-buddha or a bodhisattva and more, for the sake of rescuing these different beings. I do not only appear to them as a Buddha.

Look at me. For past infinite kalpas of lives, I have been diligently exerting various techniques to rescue those most obstinate, hard-to-tame, sinful, suffering beings[85].

However, there are still many untamed beings who will meet their retributions according to their karma. When you see them falling into the evil paths and suffering severe distress, you must remember what I am entrusting to you in this Trāyastriṃśa Palace: 'From now until *Maitreya*[86] becomes a Buddha in this mundane world, all sentient beings in this Sahā World are under your care. You are to rescue and liberate them, so that they can forever depart from suffering, and you are to continue your care until they encounter a Buddha to anoint them as future Buddhas.'"

Then, all the divided-identical Kṣitigarbha Bodhisattvas from all the different worlds reassembled into one entity. Moved by the great mercy and kindness of the Buddha as well as the grave mission entrusted upon Him, He became tearful and said to the Buddha:

[Promises and Vows of Kṣitigarbha Bodhisattva]

"For long kalpas of time, I have been guided and empowered by the Buddhas, and I have gained inconceivable miraculous power along with great wisdom. My transformational bodies fill the worlds, as many as there are sand grains in hundreds of thousands of myriads of millions of Ganges Rivers. In each world, I have transformed myself into hundreds of thousands of myriads of millions of entities, and each entity has delivered hundreds of thousands of myriads of millions of beings, leading them to take respectful homage in the Three Jewels, to leave forever the bitter sea of birth-and-death and to obtain the [true] happiness of *nirvāṇa*[87].

For any sentient being who performs virtuous deeds as instructed by the Three Jewels, even if the deeds are as small as a strand of hair, a droplet of water, a grain of sand, a mote of dust or even as tiny as the tip of a hair, I will make use of that little virtue, and I will let it grow in order to gain liberation and great benefits for that being. Therefore, I pray that you, Bhagavat, will not worry about those beings of future generations who commit evil deeds."

He repeated [His promise and vow] three times to the Buddha, "I pray that you, Bhagavat, will not worry about those beings of future generations with evil deeds [because I will help them gain liberation]."

At that time, the Buddha praised Kṣitigarbha Bodhisattva, "Wonderful! Wonderful! I shall support you with great joy. You will succeed in those great vows that you have been making for long kalpas of time. When all beings with evil deeds are rescued, then it will be time for you to validate the Bodhi."

CHAPTER 3

Contemplating the Karmic Deeds and Conditions of Sentient Beings

[Lady Māyā's Worry]

At that time, the Buddha's mundane mother, Lady Māyā, respectfully brought her palms together in front of her chest and asked Kṣitigarbha Bodhisattva: "O Holy One, when sentient beings in Jambudvīpa commit various karmic deeds, how different in severity are the deeds? And what kinds of retributions will these sentient beings receive?"

Kṣitigarbha replied: "Within tens of millions of worlds and regions, some have hells, and some do not; some have women, and some do not[88]; some have Buddha-dharma, and some do not[89]. Likewise, some worlds have śrāvakas and pratyeka-buddhas, and some do not[90]. [The differences in deeds committed by all sentient beings vary greatly; therefore] hell is not the only retribution for their deeds."

Lady Māyā [was still very concerned and] asked the Bodhisattva again: "I would like to know: if sentient beings in Jambudvīpa commit sinful deeds, what kinds of retributions will they receive, and what kinds of evil realms are manifested by their sinful karma?"

Kṣitigarbha replied: "Noble Mother, I hope you will listen and believe what you are about to hear. I will give you an overview."

The Buddha's mundane mother said: "Yes, I wish that you, O Holy One, will speak of this."

[*The Five Unremitting Sins*]

Then, Kṣitigarbha Bodhisattva said to the Noble Mother: "In southern Jambudvīpa, the five evil deeds that will attract grave retributions are as follows:

[The first kind of evil deed:] for those sentient beings that are not filial towards their parents, perhaps even going to the extreme of killing them, such sinful deeds will cause the beings to [magnetize and] fall into [the evil state of] Unremitting Hell for tens of thousands of millions upon millions of kalpas without an acquittal or date of release.

[The second kind of evil deed:] for those sentient beings that shed the blood of a Buddha, slander the Three Jewels or slight the sūtras [or dharma taught by the Buddha], such evil deeds will also cause the beings to [magnetize and] fall into [the evil state of] Unremitting Hell for tens of thousands of millions upon millions of kalpas without an acquittal or date of release.

[The third kind of evil deed:] for those sentient beings that invade or harm resident practitioners, blemish monks or nuns, indulge in and commit sexual misconduct in the saṃgha[91], or kill or harm a monk or nun, such beings will [magnetize and] fall into [the evil state of] Unremitting Hell for tens of thousands of millions upon millions of kalpas without an acquittal or date of release.

[The fourth kind of evil deed:] for those sentient beings who pretend that they are *śramaṇas*[92] but are not śramaṇas at heart[93]—they misuse the necessities of a Buddhist establishment, cheat lay Buddhists, violate the disciplines and commit all kinds of evil deeds—such beings will [magnetize and] fall into [the evil state of] Unremitting Hell for tens of thousands of millions upon millions

   The Sutra of Kṣitigarbha's Fundamental Vows

of kalpas without an acquittal or date of release.

[The fifth kind of evil deed:] for those sentient beings who steal the wealth, goods, grain, rice, food, drink, clothing or even one [trivial] item from the resident practitioners, such acts of stealing will cause the beings to [attract and] fall into [the evil state of] Unremitting Hell for tens of thousands of millions upon millions of kalpas without an acquittal or date of release."

Kṣitigarbha continued: "Noble Mother, if any sentient beings commit the above-mentioned five sinful deeds, they will certainly fall into the Five Unremitting Hells as a consequence, where they cannot even plead for an instance of relief from the suffering."

Again, Lady Māyā addressed Kṣitigarbha Bodhisattva, asking: "Why is it called Unremitting Hell?"

[Unremitting Hell]

Kṣitigarbha replied: "Noble Mother, all the hells are located within the Great Iron-Enclosed Mountains. There are eighteen large, major hells, and there are five hundred secondary hells, each with its own name, and again, there are hundreds of thousands of more hells whose names are also different.

The exterior of the major hells has walls with a circumference of more than forty thousand kilometers and a height of five thousand kilometers. The walls are made of solid iron and covered with fire, which burns in all spaces and spares none. Within the fiery walls, there are many hells. Although all the hells are connected with each other, each has its own name.

There is only one hell called Unremitting. The circumference of its walls is nine thousand kilometers and the height is five hundred kilometers. The walls are also made of solid iron. Fiery flames shoot down from the top towards the bottom, and from the bottom towards the top [covering the entire wall]. There are iron serpents and iron hounds patrolling and galloping back and forth across the top of the wall, breathing out fiery flames [to drive back in those trying to escape].

Within Unremitting Hell, there is a huge bed covering an area of five thousand kilometers. When a sinful being is enduring suffering, he only sees himself tied to the bed all alone, with his body stretched out, covering the entire bed. Though there are tens of millions of beings enduring the same suffering, each one only sees himself stretched out and covering the entire bed.

These manifestations are the retributions from committing the Five Unremitting sins.

These sinful beings must further endure enormous sufferings. There are hundreds of thousands of yakṣas and evil ghosts with teeth protruding like sharp and long swords; their eyes are intimidating, like lightning flashes. They have copper claws growing on their hands, and they drag, snatch, pull and seize these sinful beings.

Moreover, there are yakṣas holding big iron forks, spearing at the torsos of those sinful beings, or at their mouths or noses, or their bellies or backs, hurling them into the air repeatedly, or throwing them onto the bed.

There are iron eagles pecking out and devouring the eyes of these sinful beings. There are iron serpents strangling their necks. There are yakṣas driving long nails into hundreds of joints of each of these sinful beings, pulling out their tongues and letting

	The Sutra of Ksitigarbha's Fundamental Vows

iron cows plough them, and their intestines are ripped out and chopped to pieces. Melted copper is poured into their mouths, and their bodies are entwined with hot iron.

Any one of these tortures could cause an immediate death, but the dead will soon be reborn again for tens of thousands of times [to experience further tortures]. Whoever has committed the Five Unremitting Sins will magnetize the manifestation of sufferings in Unremitting Hell, and for hundreds of millions of kalpas, they will have no chance to get out.

[Worst of all, the sinful retribution for Unremitting Hell has no end to it.] When this realm comes to a total destruction, the hell beings will transmigrate to another realm [to continue the sufferings]; when that realm also comes to a total destruction, the hell beings will relocate to yet another realm; and when that realm comes to its destruction, the hell beings will transmigrate yet again, and again. When this realm comes into formation once more, the hell beings will return. [Any of the Unremitting Hells has strong magnetizing forces for sentient beings who have committed the Five Rebellious Grave Sins[94].] The unremitting sinful retributions are thus."

[Five Manifestations Constituting Unremitting Hell]

[Kṣitigarbha Bodhisattva continued:] "Furthermore, there are five manifestations induced by karmic deeds; therefore, they are called 'Unremitting'. What are the five?

First [manifestation is time]—every moment, day and night, is suffering that lasts for kalpas without a moment of rest. Therefore, it is called Unremitting.

Second [manifestation is space]—the space can be entirely filled by one sentient being or by many beings [without leaving any extra space]. Therefore, it is called Unremitting.

Third [manifestation is torturing]—the instruments of torture are used in turn repeatedly such as forks, clubs, eagles, serpents, wolves, hounds, pestles, millstones, saws, chisels, files, axes, cauldrons with boiling liquid, iron nets, iron ropes, iron donkeys, iron horses; rawhide halters bound around the head; hot iron poured over the body; gulping iron pellets when hungry; and drinking melted hot iron when thirsty. The miserable suffering continues year after year, kalpa after kalpa, up to nayuta kalpas without an end. That is the reason for the term Unremitting.

Fourth [manifestation is of no exception]—regardless whether one is a man or woman, a certain ethnic group, race or nationality, young or old, noble or indigent, a nāga, a god, a deva or a ghost, as long as one has committed the deed of the Five Unremitting Sins, one has to suffer these tortures without exception. Because there is no exception, the hell is thus called Unremitting.

Fifth [manifestation is of unremitting deaths and rebirths]— once a sentient being falls into this hell, from the time of entering the hell for hundreds of thousands of kalpas, he or she has to go through all the sufferings moment to moment, even after dying and being reborn tens of thousands of times within one day and one night. There is no hope to get even an instance of pause from the suffering, unless one atones for the sinful, karmic deeds and becomes reborn elsewhere. Such continuous and unremitting births and deaths is thus called Unremitting."

Kṣitigarbha Bodhisattva told the Noble Mother: "I am only giving a very simple and general description of Unremitting Hell.

   The Sutra of Ksitigarbha's Fundamental Vows

If I were to speak of all the hells and all the sufferings within them, including all the devices of torture and the torture methods, my narration would still be incomplete even after a kalpa of time."

After hearing these miserable recounts, Lady Māyā was most worried and saddened. With palms together, she made obeisance and withdrew.

CHAPTER 4

Magnetized Karmic Retributions of Sentient Beings in Jambudvīpa

[Empowerment and Entrustment]

At that time, Kṣitigarbha Bodhisattva Mahāsattva said to the Buddha: "O Bhagavat! I have been empowered by the miraculous powers of all the Buddha-Tathāgatas, thus I have been able to divide and transform myself throughout over hundreds of thousands of myriads of millions of worlds, into so many reproduced entities, for the sole purpose of rescuing all sentient beings who were receiving their karmic retributions. Without Tathāgata's great miraculous power, profound kindness and mercy, I would not be able to perform so many miraculous changes [nor possess such great capacity to perform these miraculous deeds].

Now I am honored to be delegated by you, Buddha, to liberate all sinful-suffering beings in the six realms, from now until *Ajita*[95] achieves Buddhahood as you, Bhagavat, have entrusted. I will carry out the task faithfully. Please do not worry."

[The Karmic Path]

Then, the Buddha told Kṣitigarbha Bodhisattva: "Before all those sentient beings gain their deliverance, [the forces of evil and virtue within their minds are in a constant tug of war because] they lack firm disposition and direction. If habitually they lean towards the evil direction, they will tend to attract evil conditions and commit evil karmic deeds. If they habitually lean towards the virtuous direction, they will attract virtuous deeds and obtain innumerable virtuous consequences. Nevertheless, all sentient beings are at all times influenced by their environments and are being drawn [by the *collective karma-fields*[96]] to do virtuous or evil deeds.

Therefore, all sentient beings are continuously reincarnating among the five paths[97] without a moment of rest. After numerous kalpas—as many as all the dust particles added together—have passed, their minds remain confused with obstinate barriers.

The situation is very much like a fish caught by fish nets. In a long river or stream, the fish might seem to have ample space to swim freely, but [the truth is] once the fish strives and succeeds to free itself from one net, it soon becomes trapped in another net. The escape is only momentary. These kinds of sentient beings are my great concern.

However, since you are going to fulfill the profound vows that you have asserted over numerous kalpas and will surely and extensively rescue those sinful-suffering beings, I need not worry!"

[*The Vow of a King—Another Past Life of Kṣitigarbha Bodhisattva*]

As these words were said, in the assembly there was a Bodhisattva Mahāsattva named *Samādhi Self-at-Ease King* (*Samādhīśvara-rāja*) who asked the Buddha: "Bhagavat! What kinds of vows has Kṣitigarbha Bodhisattva made in those numerous kalpas, so that He receives Bhagavat's repeated and immense praise and acclamation? Please, Bhagavat, give us a brief description!"

Then, Bhagavat said to *Samādhi Self-at-Ease King Bodhisattva*: "Listen attentively! Listen clearly! And contemplate further the profound meanings of the vows that I am about to explain for you one by one.

   The Sutra of Kṣitigarbha's Fundamental Vows

One time, infinite asaṃkhyeya, nayuta and unspeakable numbers of kalpas ago, there was a Buddha bearing the name *All Wisdom Accomplished Tathāgata (Sarvajña-siddhārtha)* [who had the ten meritorious designations[98]]:

Arhat—[One who is worthy.]

Samyak-saṃbuddha—[One of perfect and complete enlightenment.]

Vidyā-caraṇa-saṃpanna—[One who is endowed with complete wisdom and perfect practice.]

Sugata—[One who is well-gone.]

Lokavid—[One who is knower of the mundane world.]

Anuttara—[One who is unsurpassed.]

Puruṣa-damya-sārathi—[One who is the leader of the caravan of men to be tamed and converted.]

Śasta-deva-manuṣyāṇām—[One who is the greatest mentor of all humans and celestial beings.]

Buddha—[The Enlightened One.]

Bhagavat—[The Most Venerable and Blessed One.]

[From the time He made His presence in the world until He entered nirvāṇa,] that Buddha had a lifespan of sixty thousand kalpas.

Before he left all his mundane attachments to become a monk, he was the king[99] of a small nation. He befriended another king of a neighboring kingdom. Both of them upheld and practiced the *Ten Virtuous Disciplines*[100], and at the same time they governed and promoted the Ten Virtuous Disciplines amongst their people for the sake of everyone's well-being. [Such efforts also advanced their own merits.]

Nevertheless, the people of other neighboring countries practiced evil ways. The two kings held counsel and discussed their concern. They came up with plans to offer vast and convenient ways [to rescue those sentient beings who had committed evil deeds].

The first king made the vow: 'I will validate Buddhahood as soon as possible, so I can rescue all those sinful-suffering beings without leaving anyone behind.'

The second king made the vow: 'I will not pursue directly the path of becoming a Buddha until I have helped all sinful-suffering beings to attain peace and happiness, and ultimately achieve *Bodhi*[101].'"

The Buddha told *Samādhi Self-at-Ease King Bodhisattva*: "The first king, who vowed to achieve Buddhahood as soon as possible, is *All Wisdom Accomplished Tathāgata*. The second king, who vowed to rescue all sinful-suffering beings and not become a Buddha until he accomplished his vow, is Kṣitigarbha Bodhisattva."

[*The Vow of Bright-Eyes Girl—Another Past Life of Kṣitigarbha Bodhisattva*]

[Bhagavat continued:] "Again in the past, infinite asaṃkhyeya kalpas ago, there was a Buddha who appeared in the world bearing the name *Pure Lotus Eye Tathāgata* (*Viśuddhi-padma-cakṣu*), who had a lifespan of forty kalpas.

[After *Pure Lotus Eye Tathāgata* went into nirvāṇa] during the Dharma-Resemblance Period, there was an Arhat who applied his meritorious means to save sentient beings according to their readiness to respond to the teaching.

     The Sutra of Kṣitigarbha's Fundamental Vows

He met a woman named Bright-Eyes (*Prabhā-cakṣu*) who made the offering of food. He asked Bright-Eyes: 'What is your wish?' Bright-Eyes answered: 'Since the day my mother passed away, I have been making monetary offerings to the Three Jewels, hoping to cultivate a vast field of merits to rescue my mother. Yet, I have no way of knowing which realm she has reincarnated into.'

The Arhat felt empathy and mercy for her and focused his mind with profound concentration (*samādhi*). He saw that the mother of Bright-Eyes had fallen into an evil realm, and she was enduring great pain.

He [came out of his meditative state and] asked Bright-Eyes: 'What evil deeds did your mother commit while alive? What caused her to fall into an evil realm and suffer great pain?'

Bright-Eyes answered: 'When my mother was alive, she was fond of eating [live] fish and turtles, especially their roe and eggs. She indulged in eating them either fried or boiled. Therefore, the actual number of lives she took was tens of millions of times that of the number of [live] animals she ate. Honorable Yours! Please have kindness and mercy upon me. Please tell me what I shall do to rescue her.'

The Arhat was touched and thought of a convenient way to assist her. He advised: 'Make a sincere vow that you will chant and contemplate the name and the merits of *Pure Lotus Eye Tathāgata*. Also, sculpt or draw His image. Such efforts will have beneficial returns for both the deceased and the living.'

After Bright-Eyes heard this, she promptly relinquished all her beloved possessions to have the Buddha's image painted right away and made offerings to the Buddha. Then, with an utmost reverent mind, she gazed and paid obeisance with sobbing grief.

Unexpectedly, at night during her sleep, she dreamed of seeing *Pure Lotus Eye Tathāgata*, whose body, as tall as Mount Sumeru, was covered in golden rays and emitted brilliant lights. He said to Bright-Eyes: 'Very soon, your mother will be reborn into your household. As soon as the baby can feel hunger and cold, it will be able to speak.'

Shortly thereafter, a servant girl in the house gave birth to a baby who began to speak before it was three days old. The baby bowed in tears and told Bright-Eyes with great sadness and pain: 'All mundane people [regardless of who they are] must endure all the consequences of the karmic deeds that they have committed between births and deaths. I am your deceased mother. Since I left you, I have stayed too long in a very dark place, and I have repeatedly fallen into large hells. Fortunately, you have been cultivating blessings [by making offerings to honor the Three Jewels and the Arhat]. Relying on your meritorious power, I was able to leave the realm of hells and be reborn as a human, but only one of low class with a short lifespan. I will die at thirteen years of age and will reincarnate again and again in the three evil realms. Do you have any plan to spare me from these sufferings and emancipate me?'

Upon hearing these words, Bright-Eyes felt, without a doubt, that the baby was indeed her mother. She sobbed with great grief and said to the baby of the servant girl: 'Since you are my deceased mother, you should know what basic evil deeds you committed as a human, and which deeds caused you to fall into the evil realm.'

The baby of the servant girl answered: 'The two evil deeds that I committed were killing and the use of insulting, harmful

   The Sutra of Kṣitigarbha's Fundamental Vows

speech. Because of these grave karmic deeds, I have been suffering retributions. Without your meritorious power to pull me out of my suffering, I would have continued to stay in that great hell, receiving evil retributions without any chance for release.'

Bright-Eyes asked: 'Can you describe the retributions that you suffered in hell?'

The baby of the servant girl sighed: 'The sufferings endured because of my sins are unbearable to recall. If you insist on having me describe them, I would not be able to tell them all even in hundreds of thousands of years.'

Hearing these words, Bright-Eyes cried even more profusely, to the point of howling with grief. Then she turned her face upward and pledged into space: 'I wish that my mother will forever stay away from hells. I wish that after this child dies at age thirteen, all the grave sins from my mother's past lives will be eradicated and she will never reincarnate into the three evil realms again. All the Buddhas in the ten directions [of this universe], please shed your great kindness and mercy upon me, and witness the grand vow that I am about to make for the salvation of my mother—

If my mother can forever depart from the three evil realms, low class status, or even womanhood, then I will make this grand vow in front of the image of *Pure Lotus Eye Tathāgata*: "I vow from this day on, throughout hundreds of thousands of myriads of millions of kalpas, that I will rescue all sinful-suffering beings in those worlds that have hells as well as the lower three realms. I vow to help them leave all hells, the animal realm and the realm of hungry ghosts. Only after those receiving retribution for their sins [take reliance in the Three Jewels, cultivate the Buddha's way and] become Buddhas, will I then become a Buddha."'

After making this profound vow, Bright-Eyes heard *Pure Lotus Eye Tathāgata* respond: 'Bright-Eyes, you have great kindness and mercy to make such a grand vow on behalf of your mother. From what I see with my Buddha's vision, after your mother passes away at age thirteen, all her past sinful deeds and evil retributions will be renounced. She will be reborn as a Buddhist practitioner (*brahmacārī*[102]) with a lifespan of one hundred years. After that, she will be reborn into the *Worry-Free World* (*Aśoka*) with a lifespan of infinite kalpas. Finally, she will achieve Buddhahood and rescue human and celestial beings as numerous as the sand grains in the Ganges River.'"

The Buddha told *Samādhi Self-at-Ease King*: "The Arhat, who rescued Bright-Eyes with his meritorious power, is now Inexhaustible-Awareness Bodhisattva (*Akṣayamati*). The mother of Bright-Eyes is now Liberation Bodhisattva (*Mokśa*). Bright-Eyes is now Kṣitigarbha Bodhisattva. From past infinite kalpas onward, He has applied so much kindness and mercy, with as many long-lasting grand vows as there are sand grains in the Ganges River, to prevalently rescue all sinful-suffering beings."

[Liberated from Evil Destiny]

[The Buddha continued:] "In the future, if there are men and women who:

Fail to practice virtuous deeds; or
Succumb to evil ones; even
Disbelieve the Law of Cause and Consequence; or
Practice sexual misconduct[103] and use deceptive
    speech, or
Use alienating speech[104] and ill-intended speech; or
Slander the *Mahāyāna* (Great Vehicle)[105],

                    The Sutra of Kṣitigarbha's Fundamental Vows

Those sentient beings who have committed these deeds will certainly fall into the evil realms.

If they come across a true, virtuous mentor who can give advice and guidance so they can, as instantly as snapping one's finger, take homage in Kṣitigarbha Bodhisattva, they can be immediately liberated from the retributions of the three evil realms.

If these beings can further:

Pledge their utmost reliance [in Kṣitigarbha Bodhisattva];
Pay their respect by saluting or gazing upon His image;
Chant His name and praise His merits; and also
Make offerings with incense, flowers, clothing, jewels,
    food and drink,

With these respectful practices, for the future hundreds of thousands of myriads of millions of kalpas, they will be born into the realm of celestial beings, enjoying supreme happiness.

Even if their blessings as celestial beings come to an end, they can be reborn in the human realm for hundreds of thousands of kalpas, often as worldly leaders. They shall possess the wisdom to recall their past lives—the causes and consequences from beginning to end."

[Entrusting this Sūtra]

"O, *Samādhi Self-at-Ease King*! This Kṣitigarbha Bodhisattva has such inconceivable, enormous, powerful, miraculous strength that He can profusely and extensively benefit sentient beings. You and the rest of the Bodhisattvas should designate this *Sūtra*[106]— extensively advocate, circulate and teach it in the future."

Samādhi Self-at-Ease King said to the Buddha: "Bhagavat, please do not worry. We, the tens of thousands of millions upon millions of Bodhisattva Mahāsattvas, will definitely be empowered by the Buddha's great, miraculous strength to expound this Sūtra extensively to benefit those sentient beings in Jambudvīpa."

After *Samādhi Self-at-Ease King Bodhisattva* made such a vow in front of the Bhagavat, he reverently brought his palms together, made obeisance and withdrew.

[*Rescuing Beings Who Have Committed Evil Deeds*]

Then, the Celestial Kings of the Four Directions[107] stood up, reverently brought their palms together and addressed the Buddha: "Bhagavat, from distant kalpas ago, Kṣitigarbha Bodhisattva has been making such grand vows. Why has He not finished His work of saving those beings, and why does He still need to reinforce His grand vows again? Please, Bhagavat, we solely wish that you would explain this to us."

The Buddha told the Four Celestial Kings: "Very well! Very well! In order to be of great benefit, I will now tell you and all beings in the human and celestial realms of the present and future how Kṣitigarbha Bodhisattva, with His immense kindness and mercy, rescues all sinful-suffering beings in Jambudvīpa of the Sahā World who are trapped on the revolving path of births-and-deaths. I will also tell of the convenient techniques that He applies."

The Four Celestial Kings said: "Yes, Bhagavat, we would be pleased to hear!"

The Buddha told the Four Celestial Kings: "From distant

   The Sutra of Ksitigarbha's Fundamental Vows

kalpas ago until now, Kṣitigarbha Bodhisattva has been rescuing and liberating sentient beings. Yet, His vows are still not fully completed.

He is most kind and merciful towards the sinful-suffering beings of this world. Furthermore, He sees that, in the infinite future kalpas [and the fact that all beings will still manufacture evil deeds and suffer karmic retributions], the situation is like a creeping vine which will grow and branch out without end. Therefore, Kṣitigarbha Bodhisattva needs to reinforce His profound vows again and again. He continues to apply hundreds of thousands of myriads of millions of convenient means to teach, guide and transform all sinful-suffering beings in Jambudvīpa of the Sahā World.

O, Four Celestial Kings! Kṣitigarbha Bodhisattva [reveals the following convenient and tactful techniques of cause, condition, consequence and retribution to transform and rescue those beings with evil deeds]:

if encountering those who kill, He reveals that the retributions are to suffer ill fate and have a short lifespan [as well as encounter disasters and suffer frequent illnesses[108]];

if encountering those who steal, He reveals that the retributions are to suffer poverty and hardships;

if encountering those who commit sexual misconduct, He reveals that the retribution is to be reborn as magpies, pigeons or mandarin ducks[109];

if encountering those who use harsh and harmful speech, He reveals that the retribution is to have quarrelsome dependents within the family or clan [that lack peace and harmony];

if encountering those who slander, insult and smear others, He reveals that the retribution is to become mute or have painful, malignant sores in the mouth;

if encountering those who are hateful and angry, He reveals that the retribution is to have unsightly appearances as hunchbacks or handicapped;

if encountering those who are stingy, He reveals that the retribution is to have unfulfilled wishes or contrary outcomes;

if encountering those who are indulgent in eating and drinking, He reveals that the retribution is to live in hunger and thirst or have a disease that blocks proper intake of food and drink;

if encountering those who indulge in hunting and catching animals, He reveals that the retribution is to meet their own deaths with shocking bewilderment and extreme fear;

if encountering those who are unfilial and rebellious to their parents, He reveals that the retribution is to meet their deaths by natural calamities or accidents;

if encountering those who set fire to a forest, He reveals that the retribution is to meet their deaths in frenzied confusion, like animals running amidst a forest fire;

if encountering those parents and step-parents who are vicious [in mistreating their children or step-children], He reveals that the retribution is to be whipped and flogged in their future lives;

if encountering those who poach the new born or young[110], He reveals that the retribution is to be painfully separated from their blood relatives;

   The Sutra of Ksitigarbha's Fundamental Vows

if encountering those who slander the Three Jewels, He reveals that the retribution is to become blind, deaf, mute or hoarse in speech;

if encountering those who belittle the dharma and disrespect the teachings, He reveals that the retribution is to live forever in evil realms;

if encountering those who sabotage and take possession of the necessities from the saṃgha, He reveals that the retribution is to be reincarnated in hells for hundreds of millions of kalpas;

if encountering those who insult and smear practitioners or the saṃgha, He reveals that the retribution is to be forever reincarnated in the animal realm;

if encountering those who scald with hot water or oil, burn, hack or cut other beings with sharp objects, He reveals that the retribution is to be treated the same way in their future reincarnations;

if encountering those who break the regulations of abstinence and disregard fasting rules of their own beliefs or those of others, He reveals that the retribution is to fall into the path of fowls and animals to suffer constant hunger;

if encountering those who irrationally waste or destroy resources, He reveals that the retribution is that whenever they have urgent needs, either supply is unavailable or assistance not given;

if encountering those who are arrogant and uphold self-importance, He reveals that the retributions are to carry out inferior duties and to be despised by others frequently;

if encountering those who create confusion and contention among others with alienating speech, He reveals that the retribution is to become mute or have a hundred tongues[111];

if encountering those who hold erroneous views, He reveals that the retribution is to be reincarnated in a desolate region [with minimal chance to learn about the Three Jewels]."

[The Buddha continued: "On behalf of Kṣitigarbha Bodhisattva, I am disclosing the relationships of causes and consequences regarding how] those sentient beings in Jambudvīpa, because of their deeds of action, speech and thought, will suffer the evil retributions in hundreds of thousands of ways. [O, Four Celestial Kings! Please understand] I am only giving general descriptions.

Because sentient beings in Jambudvīpa vary in their offenses, the retributions called for by various deeds are different, and Kṣitigarbha Bodhisattva directly applies hundreds of thousands of convenient techniques to teach and transform them.

These sentient beings must receive these retributions first, and then fall into hells to receive further retributions. Even after kalpas of time have elapsed, they are still unable to become liberated.

Therefore, Four Celestial Kings! Your responsibility is to protect these humans and their countries. Do not let these sentient beings get further deluded and trapped by those evil deeds."

After hearing the Buddha's teaching, the Four Celestial Kings, in tears and sadness, reverently brought their palms together in front of their chests, made obeisance and withdrew.

     The Sutra of Kṣitigarbha's Fundamental Vows

CHAPTER 5

Names of the Hells

[Purpose of Discussing Various Hells]

At that time, *Samantabhadra* (Universal Worthy) *Bodhisattva Mahāsattva*[112] addressed Kṣitigarbha Bodhisattva:

"Your Kindness! For the sake of devas, nāgas and the four groups [of Buddha's disciples—bhikṣus, bhikṣuṇīs, upāsakas, upāsikās—] as well as all sentient beings of the present and future, may you speak of the places where sinful-suffering beings of the Sahā World and Jambudvīpa will receive their retribution, such as the names of the hells[113] and the kinds of suffering they will endure. This will allow the beings in the Dharma-Declining Period to [be alerted with heightened consciousness and] know the consequences [of their action, speech and thought]."

Kṣitigarbha replied: "Your Kindness! With the empowerment from the Buddha's majestic, miraculous strength and that of yours, Mahāsattva, I will briefly talk about the names of the hells, the sins that lead to the retributions, and the evils that lead to the sufferings."

[Names of the Hells]

"Your Kindness! In the east of Jambudvīpa are the Iron-Enclosed Mountains. They are dark and deep, where sunshine and moonlight cannot reach. Within the Iron-Enclosed Mountains, there is a major hell called Extreme Unremitting (*Avīci*) and another hell called *Mahāvīci*.

And still, there is another hell called Four-Corners;
and still, there is another hell called Flying-Swords;
and still, there is another hell called Flaming-Arrows;
and still, there is another hell called Compressing-Mountains;
and still, there is another hell called Piercing-Spears;
and still, there is another hell called Iron-Carts;
and still, there is another hell called Iron-Beds;
and still, there is another hell called Iron-Cattle;
and still, there is another hell called Iron-Bodysuits;
and still, there is another hell called Thousand-Blades;
and still, there is another hell called Iron-Donkeys;
and still, there is another hell called Molten-Copper;
and still, there is another hell called Embracing-Pillars;
and still, there is another hell called Flowing-Lava;
and still, there is another hell called Tongue-Plowing;
and still, there is another hell called Head-Filing;
and still, there is another hell called Foot-Scorching;
and still, there is another hell called Eye-Pecking;
and still, there is another hell called Iron-Balls;
and still, there is another hell called Endless-Dispute;
and still, there is another hell called Iron-Hatchet;
and still, there is another hell called Much-Hatred."

Kṣitigarbha said: "Your Kindness! Within the Iron-Enclosed Mountains there are such hells, endless in number. [Besides those already spoken of,] there are also:

Howling Hell[114];
Tongue-Pulling Hell;
Excretion Hell;
Copper-Lock Hell;
Flaming-Elephant Hell;
Flaming-Hound Hell;

     The Sutra of Kṣitigarbha's Fundamental Vows

Flaming-Horse Hell;
Flaming-Cattle Hell;
Flaming-Mountain Hell;
Flaming-Stone Hell;
Flaming-Bed Hell;
Flaming-Beam Hell;
Flaming-Hawk Hell;
Teeth-Sawing Hell;
Skin-Peeling Hell;
Blood-Sucking Hell;
Hand-Burning Hell;
Foot-Scorching Hell;
Hell of Inverse-Thorns;
Hell of Flaming-Houses;
Hell of Iron-Houses; and
Hell of Flaming-Wolves.

Within each of these hells, there are many smaller ones—one or two in some, three or four in others, and even hundreds of thousands in a few. Each has a different name."

[*The Karmic Forces of Our Sinful-Evil Deeds*]

Kṣitigarbha Bodhisattva told Samantabhadra Bodhisattva: "Your Kindness! These hells are perceived by evildoing beings and magnetized by their karma in Southern Jambudvīpa. The karmic force is extremely powerful—its strength is hard to overcome—as high as Mount Sumeru and as deep as the deepest sea. It creates immense barriers for practitioners during their pursuit of virtuous learning.

Therefore, all you sentient beings should never overlook any evil, nor should you consider any trivial harm or petty evil as if sinless. [Even if they do not appear now] the consequences will appear when this life is over because retributions wait for you after death. Every little evil counts and will bring on suffering! Even the most intimate relationship between a father and son in the past will not be of any help; upon death, each will go their separate ways, unable to assist one another. If they happen to meet again, neither one will be willing to shoulder any burden for the other [as what awaits each of them is already overbearing].

Now, with the empowerment of the Buddha's great miraculous power, I will only briefly describe the scenes in these hells [which all sentient beings are unable to see when alive but will encounter upon their deaths]. I hope you will have the patience to hear me out."

Samantabhadra answered: "I have long known the retribution [and its cause-condition-consequence] in the three evil realms that you are going to speak about. Still, Your Kindness, I wish that you will speak of these for the sake of all sentient beings in the future Dharma-Declining Period that are practicing evil deeds. Once they hear your words, they will be alarmed and thus take homage in the Buddha[115]."

[*Suffering Scenes in the Hells*]

Kṣitigarbha said, "Your Kindness! The sinful retributions in the hells are thus:

> there could be a hell where tongues of sinful beings
>   are pulled out to be plowed by cattle;
> there could be a hell where hearts of sinful beings
>   are taken out and eaten by yakṣas;
> there could be a hell where sinful beings are cooked

in cauldrons filled with boiling liquids;
there could be a hell where sinful beings embrace
    hot, burning copper pillars;
there could be a hell where flames of fire strike
    sinful beings;
there could be a hell made of frigid ice;
there could be a hell filled with infinite feces and urine;
there could be a hell filled with flying metal caltrops
    [whirling around];
there could be a hell with flaming spears [continuously
    attacking sinful beings];
there could be a hell where heavy blows constantly
    slam the chests and backs [of sinful beings];
there could be a hell for burning the hands and feet
    [of sinful beings];
there could be a hell for strangling sinful beings
    with iron snakes;
there could be a hell for sinful beings chased by
    iron hounds; or
there could be a hell for sinful beings riding on
    iron mules.

O Your Kindness! These are the retributions, and each hell is equipped with hundreds of thousands of apparatuses and instruments of torture on the karmic paths. Only made of copper, iron, rock and fire, these four kinds of matter are manifested by the sinful beings' karmic deeds [of action, speech and thought].

If I were to speak extensively about the sinful retributions in each hell—hells that are filled with hundreds of thousands of different kinds of sufferings and tortures—how could I possibly describe such innumerable, uncountable hells in detail? "

[Finally, Kṣitigarbha said:] "Today I am empowered by the Buddha's miraculous power and your good questions to speak generally about these matters. If I were to discuss them in detail, I would not be able to finish doing so even after exhausting kalpas of time."

The Sutra of Ksitigarbha's Fundamental Vows

CHAPTER 6:
The Praises of Tathāgata

[The Regal Presence]

At that time, Bhagavat emitted brilliant lights from His entire body, which prevalently brightened the Buddha lands that are as numerous as the sand grains in hundreds of thousands of myriads of millions of Ganges Rivers. [Along with the brilliant lights] the Buddha also prevalently delivered magnificent voices to those Buddha lands to inspire all the Bodhisattvas, Mahāsattvas, devas, nāgas, ghosts, gods, humans and non-humans[116], saying:

"Today, please listen to what I am about to commend and praise Kṣitigarbha Bodhisattva Mahāsattva for: how He, in all the worlds in the ten directions of this universe, applies His inconceivable miraculous powers, kindness and mercy to rescue and protect all sinful-suffering beings. After I enter nirvāṇa, all of you—Bodhisattvas, Mahāsattvas, devas, nāgas, ghosts, gods and others—must extensively find every convenient way to protect and promote this Sūtra, so that all sentient beings in the future can achieve and validate the happiness of nirvāṇa."

After the Buddha finished these words, there was a Bodhisattva in the assembly named *Samantavipula*[117] (Universal Extensive) who brought his palms together in front of his chest, made reverent obeisance and said to the Buddha:

"Today I witness you, Bhagavat, praising Kṣitigarbha Bodhisattva for His inconceivable, great, miraculous power and immense merits. I wish wholeheartedly that you, Bhagavat, will speak and unveil for future beings in the Dharma-Declining Period about how Kṣitigarbha Bodhisattva benefits humans and celestial beings and what kinds of virtuous causes they must plant so as to receive favorable consequences. Therefore, all the devas, nāgas and others of the Eight Legions, as well as sentient beings in the future, will respectfully receive and accept your explanations."

Then, Bhagavat said to Samantavipula Bodhisattva and the four groups of the Buddha's disciples: "Listen attentively! Listen attentively! I will give you a brief account of how Kṣitigarbha Bodhisattva benefits sentient beings in the human and celestial realms with various blissful and virtuous deeds."

Samantavipula replied: "Of course, Bhagavat! That is what I am delighted to hear."

[Hearing His Name, Seeing His Image and Knowing His Merits]

The Buddha said to Samantavipula Bodhisattva: "In the future, if there are virtuous men or virtuous women who:

> *Hear the name of Kṣitigarbha Bodhisattva Mahāsattva*
> *   [as a rescuer];*
> *Bring their palms together [as a gesture of reverence];*
> *Give praises [to Kṣitigarbha for His merits and miraculous*
> *   powers];*
> *Reverently prostrate themselves [with head touching the*
> *   ground at the feet of His image]; and*
> *Gaze upon and admire His image [with longing for*
> *   salvation],*

These persons will be exonerated of all their sinful deeds committed in the past thirty kalpas.

Furthermore, Samantavipula! If there are virtuous men or

    The Sutra of Kṣitigarbha's Fundamental Vows

virtuous women who:

> *Paint the image of Kṣitigarbha Bodhisattva with color; or*
> *Sculpt His image with earth, stone, rubber, lacquer, gold,*
> *   silver, copper or iron; and then*
> *With each gaze at the image, make one obeisance,*

For one hundred lifetimes, they will reincarnate in the Thirty-Three Heavens and will never fall into the evil realms.

If their celestial blessings come to an end and they fall back to the realm of humans, they will still become kings with abundant blessings."

[*Dislike of Being a Woman*]

"If there is a woman who dislikes being born in the body of a woman, and she:

> *Wholeheartedly makes generous offerings to the*
> *   image of Kṣitigarbha Bodhisattva—*
> *   either painted ones, or sculpted ones made of*
> *   earth, stone, rubber, lacquer, copper or iron—*
> *   and if she should continue to do so,*
> *   day after day without intermission; and also*
> *Use flowers, incense, food, clothing, colorful decoration,*
> *   canopies, banners, money, jewels or any beloved objects*
> *   as offerings,*

This virtuous woman, after her retribution as a woman ends in this life, for hundreds of thousands of millions of kalpas, she will never be reborn into the worlds that have the presence of women and certainly will never be reborn as a woman again, unless she has made a great kind and merciful vow [as her willing and conscious choice] that she wishes to remain in a woman's identity in order to rescue other beings. Due to the merits gained from making offerings to Kṣitigarbha and the strength of His merits, the empowerment will enable her not to be reborn as a woman for hundreds of thousands of millions of kalpas."

[Dislike of Her Ugly Appearance]

"Furthermore, Samantavipula! If there is a woman who strongly detests her ugly appearance and is tormented by her frequent illnesses, as long as she:

> *Gazes and makes obeisance wholeheartedly to the*
> *image of Kṣitigarbha for the time span of*
> *having a meal*[118],

For tens of millions of kalpas, she will be born with perfect appearances.

If this ugly woman is not tired of being a woman, then for hundreds of thousands of myriads of millions of births she will be reborn as a noble princess, a queen, a daughter of a royal family or a daughter of a prestigious elder; and she will be graceful with excellent features[119]. Such blissful results all come from her earnest gazing and paying solemn obeisance to Kṣitigarbha Bodhisattva."

[Protection by Gods and Ghosts]

"Furthermore, Samantavipula! If any virtuous men or virtuous women who can:

> *In front of the image of the Bodhisattva—*

The Sutra of Kṣitigarbha's Fundamental Vows

Dedicate delightful music and dance,
Praise His merits with singing and chanting, and
Make offerings of fragrant incense and fresh
        flowers, even
Persuade one person or many people to do
        the same,

Such persons, in their present lifetimes and future lives, will always be guarded and protected day and night by hundreds of thousands of ghosts and gods. They will be spared from frequently hearing about any events of horror[120], and neither shall they suffer any unexpected calamities and disasters."

[*Retributions for Ridiculing Worshippers*]

"Moreover, Samantavipula! In the future, if any evil people, evil gods or evil ghosts see virtuous men or virtuous women paying homage and respect to the image of Kṣitigarbha Bodhisattva with offerings, praises, chants and gazes of admiration, and:

These evil beings become conceited by saying such efforts
        are worthless without any merit nor benefit; or
Ridicule them with a mocking laugh; or
Talk ill of them, either behind their back, or with others, or
        persuade one person or many persons to do the same; or
Even generate a slight thought of slander,

Even after one thousand Buddhas have come and gone in this present *Bhadra Kalpa*[121], these evil beings will remain in Avīci Hell to suffer severe pain [without any salvation or liberation].

After this Bhadra Kalpa has passed, these evil beings will [come out of Avīci Hell to] be reborn as Hungry Ghosts[122].

After another thousand kalpas have passed, they will be reborn as animals.

And after a thousand more kalpas have passed, they will be reborn as humans. As humans, they will belong to the lower class and suffer in poverty and will be looked down upon; they will also be handicapped, crippled and mentally disabled.

At the same time, their karmic minds will easily turn to evil directions [and doing evil deeds]. Before long, they will fall back into the lower paths again.

Therefore, Samantavipula! To ridicule other people for paying tribute and making offerings [to the image of Kṣitigarbha Bodhisattva] will have such terrible retributions, yet how much worse would it be if these people defame and degrade Kṣitigarbha Bodhisattva with additional evil views?"

[Salvation for the Terminally Ill or Those Tormented by Evil Ghosts and Gods]

"Again, Samantavipula! In the future, if there are men or women who:

> Have been bed-ridden for a long time, utterly unable to recover nor have an easy, swift death despite their wishes; or
> Have dreamed of evil ghosts and even of deceased family and relatives; or
> Have wandered onto dangerous paths [in dreams]; or
> Have often had nightmares, escorted under ghosts, roaming around [in perilous realms];
> As days, months and years go by, they [waste away and] become feeble and sickly, crying out in their sleep— [they are] miserable, wretched and unhappy.

These [miserable phenomena] reveal that the patients are still

   The Sutra of Kṣitigarbha's Fundamental Vows

engaging in karmic disputes [with *Yamarāja*[123]], and they have yet to agree on the severities of the patients' retributions, which will determine where they will reincarnate to.

Even when these patients are beyond any hope for recovery, they still refuse to let go of life [because they are terribly afraid of not knowing where death will lead to, and thus linger on indefinitely and prolong their suffering].

Men and women with mundane wisdom are unable to understand or explain the seemingly strange behavior of these patients. [They fail to empathize with these patients about their inner struggle, thus they are unable to feel the patients' suffering and fear.]

[The only correct things to do for these patients are:]

In front of the images of the Buddha and Bodhisattva,
    read this entire Sūtra one time aloud [for the
    patients to hear]; or
Gather the treasured belongings of the patients, or
    clothing, jewels, assets and houses, and
    say loudly and clearly to the patients:
    'I, so and so, on behalf of you and in front of the
    Sūtra and images, will relinquish these valuables
    to be used as offerings in order to—
    Honor this Sūtra and the images; or
    Have the Buddha and Bodhisattva's images
        sculpted; or
    Have a pagoda or a temple constructed; or
    Light an oil lamp; or
    Support the livelihood of the saṃgha.'

Repeat these statements three times to let the patients hear them, even if the patients are unconscious, or have already been dead for one, two, three, four or even seven days. [It is still beneficial to make the statements.] Just recite the statements and read this Sūtra aloud[124].

After the patients pass away, their past misfortunes and heavy sins—which may be as severe as the Five Unremitting Sins—will be eradicated forever and they will be reborn [as disciples of the Three Jewels] with the wisdom of knowing their past lives.

How much better will it be if those virtuous men or virtuous women would:

Hand-copy[125] *this Sūtra or have others hand-copy*
    this Sūtra; or
Paint or sculpt the image of this Bodhisattva or
    have others do the same,

They will gain enormous benefits."

[Benefits of Upholding and Studying This Sūtra]

"Therefore, Samantavipula! If you see a person who would:

Study and chant this Sūtra; or
Have the thought of praising and admiring
    this Sūtra; or
Generate a mind of great reverence towards
    this Sūtra,

You should find hundreds of thousands of convenient ways to persuade the person to keep up with such diligence without

          The Sutra of Ksitigarbha's Fundamental Vows

regress, so that in the future he or she will gain tens of thousands of millions upon millions of inconceivable merits."

[Benefitting Deceased Relatives]

"Again, Samantavipula! In the future, if there are men or women who while asleep dream of various ghosts, gods and other beings [such as hungry ghosts, animals or hell beings] that appear sad, weepy, distressed, in despair, anxious or frightened, these ghosts may be the deceased parents, brothers, sisters, husbands, wives or other close dependents of these men or women in this lifetime or in the past one, ten, hundred or even thousand lives [that need help]. These ghosts have stayed in the evil realms yet to gain deliverance with little hope of locating resources of blessings and strengths to rescue them out of their miserable states.

These men or women should tell the ghosts—the loved ones of their past lives—that they should rely on Tathāgata's various convenient ways to express a clear vow of wanting to depart from the evil realms.

Samantavipula! You should also use your miraculous power to guide those living relatives to [honor the following practices]:

Read this Sūtra in front of the image of the Buddha
and Bodhisattva with utmost sincerity;
Either read the Sūtra themselves or have others read
it for them at least three to seven times.

After finishing the sūtra reading, the relatives abiding in the evil realms will be liberated, and the living ones will never dream of them again."

[Benefitting Those Who Have Lost Freedom]

"Moreover, Samantavipula! In the future, there will be a great number of people born into the lower class as slaves, servants or those who have lost their freedom. If they are aware of what evil deeds they have committed in their past lives [that have caused them to lose their freedom as retribution in this lifetime], and they wish to change their destinies through repentance [so as to eradicate their past sinful deeds], they can perform the following:

> *Pay the utmost respect to Kṣitigarbha Bodhisattva by*
> *gazing upon and paying obeisance to His image;*
> *Chant the Bodhisattva's name ten thousand*
> *times within a time frame of seven days.*

Consequently, these people [that have lost their freedom will be empowered by Kṣitigarbha Bodhisattva's great vows and], upon ending this life of retribution, for tens of millions of reincarnations they will always be born in respectable and prestigious places and will never fall into the three evil realms again to endure great sufferings."

[Benefitting the New Born]

"Furthermore, Samantavipula! In the future, for all people in Jambudvīpa, such as *kṣatriyas*[126], brahmans, respectable elders, upāsakas and upāsikās, as well as foreigners and those in the lower castes, who give birth to newborn babies, either boys or girls, if their relatives would:

> *Read or chant this unbelievably powerful Sūtra on behalf of*
> *the babies within seven days of their births; and*
> *Also chant the Bodhisattva's name ten thousand times,*

     The Sutra of Ksitigarbha's Fundamental Vows

The newborn babies, either boys or girls, will be liberated from their unfortunate retributions due to past evil deeds[127], and the babies will be easy to raise and have increased longevity.

If the babies are born with blissful karma from the past, their good fortune and longevity will be increased."

[*Benefits of Observing the Ten Fasting Days*]

"Furthermore, Samantavipula! For future sentient beings [there is a fasting[128] method that can be called Kṣitigarbha's Ten Fasting Days. This means] every month [in the lunar calendar][129] on the first day, eighth day, fourteenth day, fifteenth day, eighteenth day, twenty-third, twenty-fourth, twenty-eighth and twenty-ninth days, and even the thirtieth day, committed sins are weighed to determine their severity. To observe these fasting days is especially important for sentient beings of Southern Jambudvīpa, because whenever their minds generate an idea or take any action, the idea and action are all karmic and sinful deeds.

Besides, they often [violate the Four Grave Prohibitions[130] and] indulge in killing, stealing, sexual misconduct and deceptive speech, and the total number of such sins are in the hundreds of thousands. Therefore, during these ten fasting days, if they would:

Read this Sūtra once per day in front of the images
of the Buddha, Bodhisattvas or Arhats,

Within a radius of nine miles, there will be no calamities.

Such acts will also spare all household members, young and old, from falling into evil realms in the present and for the future hundreds of thousands of years. If they would:

Read this Sūtra once on each of these ten fasting days,

All household members will not encounter any sudden illness, and they will have abundant food and clothing."

[Conclusion and Naming the Sūtra]

"Therefore, Samantavipula! All of you should know that Kṣitigarbha Bodhisattva has such enormous, unspeakable, great miraculous power that enables Him to accomplish hundreds of thousands of myriads of millions of beneficial matters. Sentient beings of Jambudvīpa have very special bonds with this Mahāsattva. If these sentient beings have:

> *Heard about the Bodhisattva's name;*
> *Seen the Bodhisattva's image; and*
> *Learned about this Sūtra—even three words, five*
> *   words, one gāthā[131] or one sentence,*

They will have superb peace and joy, and for hundreds of thousands of millions of lives in the future, they will be reborn in prestigious families with distinguished appearances."

At that time, Samantavipula Bodhisattva, after hearing the Buddha-Tathāgata give praises, commend and acclaim Kṣitigarbha Bodhisattva, [bared his right shoulder,] kneeled down [on his right knee], joined his palms together and said again to the Buddha: "Bhagavat, I have long known that this Mahāsattva has such inconceivable miraculous powers and great strength of vows. For the sake of future beings, I wish for them to know the great benefits [that Kṣitigarbha Bodhisattva's miraculous power and vows can bring to them]. Hence I [respectfully] raised those questions to Tathāgata. I will indeed wholeheartedly carry out the tasks [that you have entrusted me].

     The Sutra of Ksitigarbha's Fundamental Vows

O Bhagavat! What will be the name of this Sūtra? How shall I circulate and advocate this Sūtra?"

The Buddha told Samantavipula: "This Sūtra has three names—one name is *The Sūtra of Kṣitigarbha's Fundamental Vows*; another name is *The Sūtra of Kṣitigarbha's Fundamental Deeds*; yet another name is *The Sūtra of the Power of Kṣitigarbha's Fundamental Vows*.

This Bodhisattva has been declaring solemn vows since long kalpas ago, wishing to benefit all sentient beings. Therefore, all of you should circulate and advocate this Sūtra according to your vows."

After hearing these words, Samantavipula reverently brought his palms together, made an obeisance and withdrew.

CHAPTER 7

Benefitting the Living and the Deceased

At that time, Kṣitigarbha Bodhisattva Mahāsattva addressed the Buddha, saying, "Bhagavat! I have observed sentient beings in Jambudvīpa—as soon as a thought or an idea is instigated, their driving force is nothing but sin. Even if they have gained some temporary relief [from their sinful sufferings] along with a few benefits[132], soon after they will lose their original wish of seeking liberation. When they encounter unfavorable conditions, [they fall back into their habitual-sinful-karmic ways and let] evil thoughts grow, one after another.

These sentient beings are like those walking in a muddy swamp. Not only is each step difficult, they are also carrying heavy burdens on their backs. The deeper they are trapped, the heavier the burdens feel; until finally, they become stranded in the swamp which is dark, deep and bottomless."

[Unloading Our Burden]

"If they are fortunate to encounter a knowledgeable mentor who can take away part of the load or the entire load [that the sentient beings are burdened with], due to the great power of this knowledgeable mentor, they will be guided to stabilize their foothold and come back to a safe ground. Once stepping onto the safe path, they should make profound self-reflections [to understand how they have come to travel] upon this evil path. [In addition, they should make a vow that] they must never make the absurd choice to walk the dangerous path again, nor repeat the experience [of such sinful, evil suffering]."

[Gathering Capital for a Dying Person]

"Bhagavat! These sentient beings who are habitually inclined toward evil will always make some petty evil suddenly grow into an infinite and enormous one. Hence, while they are on the verge of death, their parents and other dependents[133] should help to gather some capital for them so they can have resources to meet the challenges of the journey ahead.

[The much-needed capital can be replenished by performing the following deeds:]

> *Hang banners, flags, umbrellas and canopies*
> *   [that glorify the merits of the Buddha] and*
> *Light candles or lamps*
> *   [that symbolize the wisdom of the Buddha]; or*
> *Read the Buddha's Sūtra aloud*
> *   [to get direction and guidance]; or*
> *Make reverent offerings to the images of the*
> *   Buddhas and the Saints*
> *   [such as Bodhisattvas, Pratyeka-buddhas*
> *   and Arhats to express desire for blessing]; even*
> *Chant the names of the Buddhas, Bodhisattvas*
> *   and Pratyeka-buddhas*
> *   [to create a channel of communication]*[134].

The reading and chanting should be done in front of the dying ones, so as to reach their ears and their minds[135].

If these dying persons committed many evil deeds [in their previous lives and in their current lifetime], then the deeds will magnetize the [three] evil realms [to become their future objective realities]. However, when their relatives and dependents cultivate

                    The Sutra of Kṣitigarbha's Fundamental Vows

these saintly causes for the dying [so that the meritorious *seeds of Bodhi*[136] are planted], these uncountable grave sins will all be eradicated."

[*The Window of Forty-Nine Days for the Newly Deceased*]

"If the relatives and dependents of the newly deceased want to do more for the deceased, they can prevalently perform additional meritorious deeds within forty-nine days of the deaths, so that the deceased will forever stay away from the evil paths, and reincarnate in human or celestial realms to enjoy superb happiness. At the same time, those relatives and dependents [who have performed the merits] will also gain infinite benefits for themselves."

[Kṣitigarbha Bodhisattva continued addressing the Buddha:] "Therefore, today in front of you, Buddha-Bhagavat, as well as the devas, nāgas and others of the Eight Legions, humans and non-humans, I am speaking out to advise all beings in Jambudvīpa: around the time of death, do not slaughter animals [as sacrificial offerings] nor seek refuge from ghosts and gods. Why is it so? Those measures will not give the dying ones the slightest help or benefit. Instead, more sinful-suffering causes and conditions would be produced, which would increase the sinful deeds of the dying ones.

Supposing there are those of the present and future who have been blessed with saintly merits to be reborn among human or celestial paths, but if, at the verge of death, their relatives commit these evil causes [for their sake], it will also cause the deceased [in their *invisible, in-between state* (*antarā-bhava*)[137]] to defend themselves and argue against these atrocities, [so-called 'good' intentions,] which delays their rebirth in blissful places.

Not to mention the newly deceased who, while alive, did not cultivate much virtuous roots [nor did they perform much virtuous deeds to rely on], thus based on their own deeds, they would naturally manifest and be reborn in the evil paths. Yet on the way, more burdensome loads of sins are added because of what the living ones have done for them. How can the living ones be so hardhearted as to make them entangled with more evils?

It is like a person who has traveled a long distance on foot for three days without any food, carrying a load of over one hundred pounds on his back [and he is about to collapse at any moment]. Then along comes another person who adds more to the load on his back. Regardless how light the new load is, to the traveler it is like adding a heavy load, which will [incapacitate him to take another step and] trap him into more helplessness and fatigue."

[Kṣitigarbha Bodhisattva continued:] "Bhagavat! I have closely observed sentient beings in Jambudvīpa: if they can follow the teachings of the Buddhas to perform some virtuous deeds, regardless how small the deeds are—even as small as a strand of hair, a droplet of water, a grain of sand or a mote of dust—this will bring benefits that they can reap in full."

[Reaffirming the Benefit]

As these words were said, there was a reputable elder named Great Eloquence (*Mahāpratibhāna*)[138] [who was a true Bodhisattva Mahāsattva]. He had been realizing and validating the *Dharma of No-Birth*[139] for a long time. He could transform himself into any identity he wished in order to enlighten and rescue all beings in the ten directions.

    The Sutra of Kṣitigarbha's Fundamental Vows

During this assembly, this Mahāsattva appeared as an elder. He reverently brought his palms together, made obeisance and asked Kṣitigarbha Bodhisattva: "O Mahāsattva! Is it really true that the deceased beings in southern Jambudvīpa will gain great benefits and emancipation if their close relatives and dependents cultivate many meritorious deeds, even providing a fasting meal, as virtuous causes on their behalf?"

Kṣitigarbha answered: "Elder! With the empowerment of the Buddha's miraculous strength, I will briefly discuss the matter for the sake of all sentient beings of the present and future.

Elder! If sentient beings of the present and future, on the day of their deaths, would:

*Hear the name of one Buddha, or one Bodhisattva,
    or one Pratyeka-buddha,*

Regardless of being sinful or not, they all will be liberated [from suffering and gain happiness]."

[Benefits of One-Seventh and Six-Sevenths]

Kṣitigarbha Bodhisattva continued: "If any men or women who, while alive, have not planted any virtuous seeds [nor made any effort to be connected with the Buddha], but instead committed many sinful deeds, upon their deaths, should their close relatives and dependents cultivate meritorious deeds to increase their bliss and benefits, one out of the seven parts of the bliss and benefits will go to the deceased, while the remaining six parts will go to the living ones [who have participated in the meritorious deeds].

Therefore, all virtuous men and virtuous women of the present and future should cultivate meritorious deeds for themselves in order to harvest every bit of the merits."

[*The Invisible, In-between Entity*]

"The Great Ghost of Impermanence (*anitya*) always arrives unexpectedly. [With his destructive power he can turn whatever we have previously considered permanent into bubbles soon to disappear. The sudden change will be most difficult for the newly deceased to adapt to the invisible, in-between state.]

This invisible, in-between entity (antarā-bhava) wanders around in total darkness, unable to foresee whether there is a blissful future ahead, or a harsh, sinful one. For the next forty-nine days after death, the entity exists like a foolish and deaf being [not knowing where to go and feeling extremely frightened, lost and anxious].

Or, this entity may show up in front of various tribunals, defending and arguing about his karmic consequences. After the final examination, he will be reborn according to his deeds [and he must comply with no chance for refusal]. Before knowing [the result], he suffers tens of millions of horrific worries and distress. How much more so if he falls into one of the evil realms!

Indeed, before the deceased have a firm place to go, from moment to moment within these forty-nine days, they are desperately longing for their blood relatives and dependents to urgently cultivate some blessings and provide virtuous strength for their sake in order to rescue them [from falling into the evil realms]. Because after these forty-nine days, [their destinations are decided, and] they can only comply with the consequences of their karma. [Once reincarnation takes place, the connections with

     The Sutra of Kṣitigarbha's Fundamental Vows

their previous lives are severed, leaving no memories of them.]

If the deceased are loaded with sinful deeds [with no help from their relatives and dependents], then for hundreds of thousands of years they will suffer [severe pain and harm] without a date of acquittal. If the deceased have committed the Five Unremitting Sins that will lead them to fall into the Great Hell, after thousands and tens of thousands of kalpas have passed, they will remain in that hell to endure numerous sufferings."

[Honoring the Three Jewels with a Fast]

"Furthermore, Elder! If the relatives and dependents of the sinful deceased person want to cultivate bliss, they can offer a fast [in honor of the Three Jewels] to acquire capital for the journey as the deceased proceed on the karmic path. While preparing the meal and cleaning up after the meal [the entire process should be observed with great reverence]:

> *Do not roughly and wastefully discard anything on*
> *the ground, such as the water after rinsing the*
> *rice or the unwanted vegetable leaves;*
> *No one should consume any food before making*
> *offerings to the Three Jewels first.*

If one does not follow the above instructions in preparing the food and is not sincere and diligent, the deceased will not receive any benefits.

Furthermore, if during the entire process, the relatives can:

> *Safeguard their minds without distraction; and*
> *Make offerings to the Buddha and Saṃgha first,*

Then the deceased will gain one part of the merits among a total of seven parts. [The relatives engaging in the process of offering will gain the other six parts.]

Therefore, Elder! If sentient beings in Jambudvīpa are willing to perform a fast as offering with utmost sincerity to honor the Buddha and saṃgha on behalf of their deceased parents and relatives, both the living and the deceased will obtain benefits."

As these words were said in the Palace of Trāyastriṃśa Heaven, the ghosts and gods of Jambudvīpa, numbering tens of thousands of millions upon millions of nayuta, all made vows to pursue boundless enlightenment. The Elder, Great Eloquence, made obeisance and withdrew.

    The Sutra of Ksitigarbha's Fundamental Vows

CHAPTER 8

Exclamations and Praises from Yamarāja and His Followers

At that time, *Yamarāja* and the countless numbers of ghost kings[140], traveling from [the eighteen major hells and crossing the three rings of oceans inside] the Iron-Enclosed Mountains, arrived at Trāyastriṃśa Palace where the Buddha held His assembly.

[The Invisible World]

Their names were:

> Vicious-Poison Ghost King,
> Many-Evils Ghost King,
> Great-Argument Ghost King,
> White-Tiger Ghost King,
> Blood-Tiger Ghost King,
> Crimson-Tiger Ghost King,
> Calamity-Spreading Ghost King,
> Flying-Body Ghost King,
> Lightning-Flash Ghost King,
> Wolf-Fang Ghost King,
> Thousand-Eyed Ghost King,
> Animal-Devouring Ghost King,
> Load-Bearing Ghost King,
> Ghost King of Wasted-Blessings[141],
> Ghost King of Disasters[142],
> Ghost King of Food[143],
> Ghost King of Wealth,
> Ghost King of Domesticated Animals,
> Ghost King of Fowl,

Ghost King of Beasts[144],
Ghost King of Phantoms,
Ghost King of Birthing[145],
Ghost King of Destiny[146],
Ghost King of Disease[147],
Ghost King of Danger[148],
Three-Eyed Ghost King,
Four-Eyed Ghost King,
Five-Eyed Ghost King[149],
Qi-li-shi Ghost King[150],
Great Qi-li-shi Ghost King,
Qi-li-cha Ghost King,
Great Qi-li-cha Ghost King,
Ana-zha Ghost King and
Great Ana-zha Ghost King.

All these great ghost kings, each along with their hundreds of thousands of subordinate minor ghost kings, take residence in Jambudvīpa. Each ghost king has his own jurisdiction of duty and authority.

These ghost kings, together with Yamarāja and relying on the Buddha's great miraculous strength as well as the empowerment of Kṣitigarbha Bodhisattva Mahāsattva, were able to come to Trāyastriṃśa. They all stood aside [ready to learn the teachings].

[Yamarāja's Question]

Then Yamarāja knelt down on his right knee, brought his palms together in front of his chest and reverently addressed the Buddha: "O Bhagavat! Today, we and all these ghost kings, due to the majestic empowerment of the Buddha and Kṣitigarbha Bodhisattva Mahāsattva, are able to attend this great assembly in

The Sutra of Kṣitigarbha's Fundamental Vows

Trāyastriṃśa; we are fortunate to have such privileged blessings. I have a few questions which puzzle me, if I may venture to ask Bhagavat. I wholeheartedly wish that you, Bhagavat, would extend your kindness and mercy to clarify and enlighten us."

The Buddha said to Yamarāja: "Please feel free to raise any questions. I will answer them."

At that time, Yamarāja admirably gazed at Bhagavat, paid obeisance and turned to look at Kṣitigarbha Bodhisattva[151]. Then he addressed the Buddha: "Bhagavat! I have observed, in the six realms, that Kṣitigarbha Bodhisattva has hundreds of thousands of ingenious and convenient ways to rescue sinful-suffering beings and never tires of any difficulties [nor refuses to answer any call]. This Mahāsattva has such inconceivable, miraculous power to perform miracles. Nevertheless, after those beings are liberated from the retributions of their sins, they soon fall back into the evil realms again.

O Bhagavat! Since this Kṣitigarbha Bodhisattva has such inconceivable, miraculous power, how could sentient beings fail to remain on the virtuous path where they would gain lasting deliverance? [Why do they repeatedly fall back into the evil realms?] I solely wish that you, Bhagavat, will kindly explain and enlighten me."

[The Obstinate, Hard-to-Tame, Habitual Evildoing, Sinful, Suffering Beings]

The Buddha told Yamarāja: "The temperaments of sentient beings of Southern Jambudvīpa are characterized by extreme stubbornness and unwillingness to yield. They are very difficult to mediate and tame.

Look at this Mahāsattva! For hundreds of thousands of kalpas, He continues to rescue them one after another [without a moment of rest], leading them to reach liberation sooner.

For those beings with grave, sinful deeds, including the ones who have fallen into the worst evil realms, this Bodhisattva uses His ingenious, convenient and miraculous power to uproot the origins of their karmic causes and help them recollect their past [so that they will know how the forces of their sinful deeds have continued to grow and expand].

Unfortunately, sentient beings of Jambudvīpa have the habit of clinging to evil and attracting evil. [The more evil they attract, the more evil they become; the more evil they become, the more suffering they must endure. It is extremely difficult to get away from the sea of suffering because the force of evil will pull them back like gravity, and] they repeatedly come in and out of those evil realms [as retributions]. Therefore, this Bodhisattva has been extremely attentive, and after infinite kalpas have passed, He still continues to rescue those beings.

[The Buddha continued with a parable:] It is like a person who has lost direction and is unable to find his way home. Mistakenly he walks onto a path of danger. Along the dangerous path, there are yakṣas, tigers, wolves, lions, lizards, snakes, vipers and scorpions. The lost person on the treacherous path is in imminent danger of being harmed by these poisonous beings.

Then a virtuous, knowledgeable guide appears who can easily remove the trickeries, dissolve the poisons and, moreover, halt and tame those yakṣas and evil beasts. By chance he encounters the lost person who is about to walk onto the dangerous path. He says: 'Goodness! Fellow! What are you doing? Why do you come to this

   The Sutra of Kṣitigarbha's Fundamental Vows

path? Do you have any extraordinary ability to handle evil and resist toxicities?'

Upon hearing these words, the lost person comes to his senses, realizing that he is on a malicious path. He stops right away and is afraid to go on. He pleads [to the virtuous, knowledgeable person] to be guided out of the path.

This virtuous, knowledgeable guide holds his hand and leads him out of this dangerous path, sparing him from the attack and harm of the vicious beings and the toxins. Once walking upon the smooth and safe path, he will have peace and happiness. The knowledgeable guide explains further: 'Whoa! Confused one! From today on, do not step on this [treacherous] path again. Anyone who enters this path will have difficulties to get out and will also lose one's life.'

After hearing this warning, the person who was lost realizes the seriousness of his error and is most grateful.

Upon parting, the knowledgeable guide advises further: 'If you come upon any relatives, friends and other travelers, either men or women, you must tell them that, on this path, there are many poisonous evils where they would lose their lives. Do not let those people [repeat what you have done, lest they] induce their own death.'

Therefore, Kṣitigarbha Bodhisattva [is this virtuous, knowledge-able guide who], with His great kindness and mercy, rescues those sinful-suffering beings so they may be reborn among human or celestial realms to enjoy superb, wonderful happiness and fortune.

Now that these sinful beings realize the suffering of the

karmic path and are rescued from it, they vow never to repeat the same experience again, just like the lost person [described in the parable] who mistakenly took the treacherous path, but fortunately encountered the virtuous and knowledgeable guide who brought him out of the danger. Because he now knows the suffering, he will never step onto the old path again.

In the future, if this lost person sees anyone about to enter the evil path, he will advise them not to. He also reminds himself of his past delusional, unclear and unwise mind [which trapped him on the evil path]. Now that he has been [led by the virtuous guide, Kṣitigarbha Bodhisattva, and is] liberated from delusion and harm, he must not fall back into the trap again.

If he falls back and steps onto the old path again, it is because he is still confused and lost and has not fully awakened from his past mistakes. It is likely he will lose his life and fall into the evil paths again.

Kṣitigarbha Bodhisattva will apply His convenient, miraculous power to liberate these confused and lost ones and lead them to be reborn among human and celestial realms. If they still tend to fall back to the old path, it is because their karmic entanglements are severe, and they will not gain liberation from their perpetual stay in hell."

[The Game Rules of Ghost Kings]

Then, Vicious-Poison Ghost King brought his palms together and reverently said to the Buddha: "Bhagavat! We ghost kings are infinite in number. In Jambudvīpa we either benefit humans or harm them[152], depending on each person's deeds.

                    The Sutra of Kṣitigarbha's Fundamental Vows

It is because of this karmic retribution that makes my subordinates travel amidst the world. They give out more harm than benefit. As they pass through people's households, cities, villages, estates and buildings, if they see any men or women [engaging in any of the following practices]:

Performing any virtuous deeds as small as a
strand of hair; even as much as
Hanging a banner [to celebrate the Buddha's
supremacy],
Putting up a canopy [as a symbol of supporting the
Three Jewels],
Making a small offering of incense or flowers
[as admiration] to the images of the Buddha
and Bodhisattva; or
Studying and reciting the Buddha's Sūtra, burning
incense as respectful offering to one sentence
or one gāthā,

We ghost kings will respect these persons like we respect the many Buddhas of the past, present and future. [At the same time] we will pass instructions onto the subordinate ghosts, those with strong powers and those overseeing the land, to protect these persons[153] lest any wicked matter, accident, illness, sudden sickness or unfortunate event come close to their homes, or worse, enter their doors to harm them."

The Buddha praised the Ghost King: "Wonderful! Wonderful! Since all you [ghost kings] and Yamarājāḥ will safeguard these virtuous men and women [who perform even a small offering to the Three Jewels], I shall ask *Lord Brahmā* and *Lord Śakra*[154] to guard and protect you."

[Do's and Don'ts at the Time of a New Birth]

As these words were said, a ghost king among the assembly named Ghost King of Destiny stood up and reverently addressed the Buddha: "Bhagavat! Being a ghost king is the consequence of my karmic deeds. My mission is to take charge of human lives in Jambudvīpa. All their births and deaths are under my jurisdiction.

My fundamental wish is to benefit all sentient beings [to have favorable births and favorable deaths. Yet, I can only respond to their evil deeds or virtuous deeds, not to their wishes. This is my karmic limitation that I cannot change]. Unfortunately, these sentient beings fail to understand my fundamental wish [and my limitations]. Therefore, their births and deaths can be undesirable and unsatisfying. Why is this so?

If people in Jambudvīpa—when giving birth, regardless if a boy or a girl, or about to give birth—could just perform virtuous deeds, it will bring benefits to the [entire] household. Naturally it will make *Lord of Land* [155] greatly pleased [and respond] by protecting the baby and the mother, bringing them immense peace and happiness as well as benefitting [other] relatives.

After the birth of a baby, the relatives:

> *Should not commit killing for the sake of providing*
> *extra nutrition for the mother; and*
> *Should not gather a large number of relatives and*
> *dependents to celebrate the birth of the baby*
> *with a banquet, loud music or indulgent drinking*
> *and meat eating.*

   The Sutra of Ksitigarbha's Fundamental Vows

Such celebration will deplete the mother and the new born baby of peace and happiness. Why is this so?

Because at the time of delivery, there are numerous evil ghosts, demons, monsters and spirits craving for the smelly blood. Even though I have dispatched Lord of Households and Lord of Land to protect and care for the baby and the mother, as well as to give them benefits of peace and happiness, the relatives, if pleased with the circumstance, should respond to Lord of Land with blissful deeds. Nevertheless, far too often they gather relatives and dependents [indulging in celebration as reciprocation. They slaughter animals to have banquets for relatives and friends]. Such offenses invite misfortune for them and also cause harm to the mother and the baby."

[At the Time of Death—Do Not Follow Deceased Relatives]

[Ghost King of Destiny continued:] "Furthermore, I wish to prevent those humans in Jambudvīpa from falling into the evil realms when they are on the verge of their deaths. At that moment, they cannot differentiate between virtue and evil, thus they are unable to cultivate any virtues [such as chanting Kṣitigarbha's or the Buddha's names] to benefit and give [themselves and] me the needed strength[156].

In addition, even [when I am trying to help] virtuous, dying persons in Jambudvīpa [they] are surrounded by hundreds of thousands of vicious ghosts and gods from the evil realms, who are there to tempt these dying ones by transforming themselves into the images of their deceased parents or relatives in order to lure them into the evil paths[157]. The temptation at such moments for those who have committed many evil deeds will be even harder to resist."

[Things to Do for Dying Relatives]

[Ghost King of Destiny continued:] "Bhagavat! The minds of these dying men or women in Jambudvīpa are delirious and dark, unable to differentiate between virtue and evil. At those moments, when their eyes turn blind and their ears turn deaf, their relatives should practice the following:

> *Make generous offerings [to the Three Jewels]; and*
> *Recite this venerable Sūtra; also*
> *Chant the names [and merits] of the Buddha and*
> *Bodhisattva.*

These good measures will provide a favorable condition to guide the dying ones away from the three evil realms and make all the demons, ghosts and gods retreat and disperse.

O Bhagavat! All sentient beings at the verge of their deaths, if they have had the chance to hear one Buddha's name, one Bodhisattva's name, or hear one gāthā or one sentence from the Mahāyāna sūtras, I have observed these humans—except for those who have committed the killing and harmful deeds of the Five Unremitting Sins—for those who have committed minor evil deeds causing them to fall into the evil realms, they will soon be liberated."

[The True Identity of Ghost King of Destiny]

[After hearing these words] the Buddha told Ghost King of Destiny: "You have an immense, kind and merciful mind, thus you have made such a great vow in order to safeguard all sentient beings during their births and deaths. In the infinite future, when men or women are at the verge of birth and death, you must not retreat from your vow. You must lead them to deliverance

          The Sutra of Ksitigarbha's Fundamental Vows

[away from evil realms], so that they can forever enjoy peace and happiness."

Ghost King of Destiny said to the Buddha: "Please do not worry. As long as I am a ghost king, from moment to moment I will be close to all sentient beings in Jambudvīpa and care for them so that they will have peace and happiness when they encounter births and deaths. However, I only wish that sentient beings at the time of their births and deaths will believe in and take my advice and act accordingly. Only then will they have deliverance and great benefits."

Then, the Buddha told Kṣitigarbha Bodhisattva: "This great Ghost King of Destiny has been a great ghost king for hundreds of thousands of lives. He has been supporting and protecting all sentient beings during their births and deaths, wishing them well. With this Mahāsattva's kind and merciful vows, he appears as a great ghost, yet he is not really a ghost.

One hundred seventy kalpas from now, he will become a Buddha. His title will be '*Formless Tathāgata*'; the kalpa will be named '*Blissful Kalpa*'; and the world he upholds will be named '*Pure-Habitat*'. This Buddha's lifespan will be uncountable kalpas.

[The Buddha concluded:] Kṣitigarbha! This great ghost king, his deeds [and merits] are thus inconceivable, and the humans and celestial beings that he has rescued are also infinite in number."

CHAPTER 9:

*Chanting the Names and Designations
of the Buddhas*[158]

At that time, Kṣitigarbha Bodhisattva Mahāsattva expressed to the Buddha: "O Bhagavat! Today I would like to disclose the ways and means, for the good of future sentient beings, of how they can obtain great benefits between their births and deaths. I solely wish that you, Bhagavat, will give me the opportunity to speak."

The Buddha told Kṣitigarbha Bodhisattva: "Now you wish to show your great kindness and mercy by speaking of the inconceivable ways and means employed to rescue all sinful-suffering beings among the six realms. This is the right time; please speak of them! I shall enter nirvāṇa soon, and I would like to see you fulfill your great vows [that you have made for past numerous kalpas. I want to entrust all sinful-suffering beings unto you. They are yours to rescue], so that I do not have to worry about all the present and future beings anymore."

Kṣitigarbha Bodhisattva addressed the Buddha: "Bhagavat! In the past, infinite asaṃkhyeya kalpas ago, a Buddha appeared in the world. His name was **Boundless Body Tathāgata (***Anantakāya*****)**[159]. If any men or women:

> *Hear the name of this Buddha; and*
> *Develop a respectful mind [towards this Buddha],*
> > *even for a brief moment,*

The persons' grave sins throughout their births and deaths, committed during [the most recent] forty kalpas, will be acquitted. Furthermore, if they:

Sculpt or paint this Buddha's image and
Make offerings and praise Him [and His merits],

They will gain limitless and boundless blessings.

Again in the past, as many kalpas as there are sand grains in the Ganges River, a Buddha appeared in the world. His name was **Precious Nature Tathāgata** (*Ratna-maya*)[160]. If any men or women:

Hear the name of this Buddha; and as quickly as
*   snapping one's fingers*
Make up their minds to take homage in Him,

They will immediately step onto the safe and unsurpassed path [of the *dharma king*[161]] and will never regress.

Again in the past, a Buddha appeared in the world. His name was **Superb Red Lotus Tathāgata** (*Padmottara*)[162]. If any men or women:

Hear the name of this Buddha; and
Let the name remain in their ears [and hearts],

They will be reborn in the *Heaven of Six Desires*[163] [to enjoy superb sensory pleasures] for a thousand lifetimes, let alone if they:

Chant [the name of this Buddha] with an intent
*   and focused mind.*

Again in the past, unspeakable-unspeakable asaṃkhyeya kalpas ago, a Buddha appeared in the world. His name was **Roaring Lion Tathāgata** (*Siṃhanāda*)[164]. If any men or women:

                    The Sutra of Kṣitigarbha's Fundamental Vows

Hear the name of this Buddha; and
Take homage in Him with a single and devoted mind,

They will encounter infinite Buddhas who will touch their heads and bestow upon them their future destinies [as Bodhisattvas and Buddhas].

Again in the past, a Buddha appeared in the world. His name was **Krakucchanda Buddha** (Firmly-Stop-Evil and Act-Virtuously)[165]. If any men or women:

Hear the name of this Buddha;
Gaze upon and pay tribute to His image wholeheartedly; or
Further, praise His merits,

These people, in the [current] Bhadra Kalpa assemblies of the Thousand Buddhas, will become *Lord Mahā-brahma*[166] and be bestowed superbly [as a future Buddha].

Again in the past, a Buddha appeared in the world. His name was *Vipaśyin Buddha* (Correct Contemplation)[167]. If any men or women:

Hear the name of this Buddha,

They will never fall into the three evil paths, and will always be born in the human path or celestial path to enjoy superb and refined bliss and happiness.

Again in the past, immeasurable kalpas ago, as many as there are sand grains in the Ganges River, a Buddha appeared in the world. His name was **Abundant Jewels Tathāgata** (*Prabhūta-ratna*)[168]. If any men or women:

Hear the name of this Buddha,

They will never fall into the evil paths, and will always be born in the celestial path to enjoy superb and refined bliss and happiness.

Again in the past, a Buddha appeared in the world. His name was **Precious Appearance Tathāgata** (*Ratna-ketu*)[169]. If any men or women:

Hear the name of this Buddha and bear a
    respectful mind,

They will validate their status as Arhats in the near future.

Again in the past, immeasurable asaṃkhyeya kalpas ago, a Buddha appeared in the world. His name was **Banner of a Monk's Robe Tathāgata** (*Kāṣāya-dhvaja*)[170]. If any men or women:

Hear the name of this Buddha,

Their grave sins committed throughout one hundred *mahā-kalpas* of births and deaths will be surmounted.

Again in the past, a Buddha appeared in the world. His name was **Great Penetration Mountain King Tathāgata** (*Mahābhijñā-parvata-rāja*)[171]. If any men or women:

Hear the name of this Buddha,

They will encounter many Buddhas, as numerous as the sand grains in the Ganges River, who will extensively teach them the dharma. Eventually, they will attain the Bodhi.

      The Sutra of Kṣitigarbha's Fundamental Vows

Again in the past, there was:

Pure Moon Buddha (*Śuddha-candra*)[172],
Mountain King Buddha (*Girirāja*),
Superb Wisdom Buddha (*Jñānābhibhū*),
Pure Name King Buddha (*Vimalakīrti-rāja*),
Wisdom Accomplished Buddha (*Jñānagra-sādhaka*),
Unsurpassed Buddha (*Anuttara*),
Wonderful Voice Buddha (*Mañjughoṣa*),
Full Moon Buddha (*Pūrṇa-candra*),
Moon Face Buddha (*Candra-mukha*)—
there were unspeakable numbers of Buddhas such as these.

O Bhagavat! If all sentient beings of the present and future, whether they are celestial beings, or humans, or men, or women, can chant even *one* of the [above mentioned] Buddhas' names, they will gain infinite merits. And how much better will it be to invoke many Buddhas' names! These sentient beings will gain great benefits while living, and at the time of their deaths, they will not fall into evil paths.

When there is a dying person in the household, if his relatives, even one of them, would loudly and reverently chant one Buddha's name in front of him, all sinful retributions of the dying person will be eradicated, except the Five Unremitting Sins.

If the person has committed the Five Unremitting Sins, the retributions for this are extremely severe and will last for hundreds of millions of kalpas without a chance of acquittal. Nevertheless, as long as someone chants the names of the Buddhas for him at the time of his death, his Five Unremitting Sins will gradually be eradicated.

And how much better will it be if a person can praise and chant the names [of the Buddhas] for the benefit of himself [long before the time of his death], which will provide infinite blessings in addition to eliminating his infinite sins."

The Sutra of Ksitigarbha's Fundamental Vows

CHAPTER 10

Comparative Merits of Dāna and the Necessary Conditions[173]

[Making a Request]

At that time, strengthened by the majestic powers of the Buddha, Kṣitigarbha Bodhisattva Mahāsattva stood up from His seat, [bared His right shoulder,] kneeled down on His right knee and brought His palms together [in front of His chest]. Reverently, He addressed the Buddha:

"O Bhagavat! I have been observing sentient beings who have been reincarnating on their karmic paths, and I appraised their meritorious blessings according to the dāna they have performed. Some exerted great effort, and some did very little. [Therefore, the blessings they received varied greatly in terms of quantity, profundity and duration.] Some of them enjoyed their blessings in only one lifetime, others enjoyed their blessings for ten lifetimes, and there were some who received great benefits for hundreds or thousands of lifetimes. What [were the causes and conditions of merits related to dāna that] would make such immense differences? I solely wish that you, Bhagavat, will explain that to me."

Then, the Buddha told Kṣitigarbha Bodhisattva: "Today in front of all the assembled beings in Trāyastriṃśa Palace, I shall speak of the spectrum of merits, from great to small, gained by various kinds of dāna in Jambudvīpa. Listen attentively! I am going to give you a basic explanation."

Kṣitigarbha said to the Buddha: "I have wondered about such matters, and I will be delighted to hear you speak of them."

[Dāna Performed by Leaders towards the Unfortunate]

The Buddha told Kṣitigarbha Bodhisattva: "In southern Jambu-dvīpa, there are kings, high officers, respectable elders, powerful kṣatriyas, reputable brahmans and others[174]. If they encounter the most unfortunate and impoverished people, including hunchbacks, the crippled, the mute, the deaf, the blind and those who are disabled or handicapped in some way, and these kings and others wish to perform dāna, they should:

> *Bear great kindness and mercy;*
> *Humble themselves with benevolent smiles on their faces;*
> *Personally and prevalently hand out alms; or*
> *Arrange representatives to perform the dāna; and*
>   *while doing so,*
> *Speak to the people with tender, comforting words,*

The benefits earned by these mundane leaders will be equivalent to the merits and benefits earned by making offerings to many Buddhas, and the abundance of the benefits will be as many as the total number of sand grains in one hundred Ganges Rivers.

Why [will practicing dāna by these mundane leaders earn them such great blessings]? It is because [through making dāna] the act provides powerful and wealthy mundane leaders an opportunity to generate a mind of great kindness towards the most destitute and impoverished [by empathizing with them without arrogance]. Therefore, they will gain such great benefits.

For hundreds of thousands of lifetimes, they will always possess the *Seven Royal Jewels*[175] [which are attributes of noble wheel-turning kings], and they will also enjoy an abundance of food and clothing [as well as other necessities of life]."

    The Sutra of Kṣitigarbha's Fundamental Vows

"Furthermore, O Kṣitigarbha! If in the future, there are kings, [high officers, respectable elders, powerful kṣatriyas,] brahmans and others who come across a Buddhist stūpa or temple, an image of a Buddha, even images of Bodhisattvas, Śrāvakas and Pratyeka-buddhas and they:

Personally get involved in arranging and making
offerings and practicing dāna,

The merits derived from performing these deeds will enable these kings and mundane leaders to become Lord Śakra for three kalpas and enjoy superb and exquisite pleasures[176]. If they can:

Attribute and share the merits and benefits [gained from
performing the dāna] with other sentient beings[177]
in the dharma realms[178] [instead of solely enjoying
the blessings themselves],

For ten kalpas, they will often become Lord Mahā-brahma [in the celestial realm]."

[Making Restorations]

"Furthermore, O Kṣitigarbha! If in the future, there are kings, [high officers, respectable elders, powerful kṣatriyas,] brahmans and others who come across old stūpas or temples of past Buddhas that are broken down and damaged, or Buddhist sūtras that are worn and torn, or images [of Buddhas, Bodhisattvas and Pratyeka-buddhas] that are poorly maintained and they:

[Make a vow to] supervise the restoration personally; or

*Persuade others, as many as hundreds of thousands of
people, to participate in this dāna and make
connections [with the Three Jewels],*

These leaders, for hundreds of thousands of lifetimes, will always be wheel-turning kings. Those participants who take part in the dāna, for hundreds of thousands of lifetimes, will always be kings of small nations [or mundane leaders].

In addition, if all of them can, in front of these restored stūpas or temples:

*Vow to attribute and share the merits and benefits with
other beings in the dharma realms,*

These kings and others will ultimately become Buddhas. The merits gained from such dāna will be countless and boundless."

[Dāna to Those in Urgent Need]

"Furthermore, O Kṣitigarbha! In the future, there are kings, [high officers, respectable elders, powerful kṣatriyas,] brahmans and others who come across the elderly, the sick or pregnant women who are about to give birth and if they, in an instant:

*Generate great kindness and
Provide [much-needed] medical care, food, drink and bedding
So that they can have peace and comfort,*

Such meritorious benefits [gained from the dāna] are most inconceivable:

*[First of all] these leaders will never fall into the evil realms,
and even*

                    The Sutra of Kṣitigarbha's Fundamental Vows

For hundreds of thousands of lifetimes, they will not hear any
    sounds of suffering;
For two hundred kalpas, they will always be celestial lords of
    the heavens of Six Desires;
For one hundred kalpas, they will always be celestial lords of
    the Pure Abode heavens[179];
Ultimately, they will become Buddhas."

[Conclusion of Leaders' Dāna]

"Therefore, Kṣitigarbha! If in the future, there are kings, [mundane leaders,] brahmans and others who can make the afore-mentioned dāna, they will gain infinite meritorious benefits. Furthermore, if they can:

> *Attribute the merits of dāna [to the past, present and*
> *   future beings in the dharma realms, instead of*
> *   enjoying the gains themselves],*
> *Regardless [the quantity of the dāna is] great or small,*

Ultimately, they will [accumulate capital to] become Buddhas, let alone wheel-turning kings, Lord Śakras and Lord Brahmās as retribution.

Therefore, Kṣitigarbha! You shall prevalently advise sentient beings [of the present and future] to learn correctly as discussed afore."

[Planting Virtuous Roots by Virtuous Men and Women]

"Furthermore, O Kṣitigarbha! In the future, if virtuous men or virtuous women:

Plant some virtuous roots[180] *when practicing and*
   upholding the Buddha-dharma,
Regardless how small the roots may be—as tiny as
   the tip of a hair, a strand of hair, a grain of sand
   or a mote of dust—

The benefits and blessings [that the virtuous men or women will enjoy] are too plentiful to calculate and describe."

[*Dāna to the Holy Images*]

"Furthermore, O Kṣitigarbha! In the future, if there are virtuous men or virtuous women who encounter images of the Buddhas, Bodhisattvas, Pratyeka-buddhas or wheel-turning kings:

Perform dāna and make offerings [as well as financially
   support the places that house these images],

Consequently, they will obtain infinite blessings. They will always be reincarnated in the realms of human and celestial beings to enjoy wonderful and superb pleasures. If they can:

Attribute the blessings to [all beings in] the dharma realms
   [instead of claiming the blessings personally],

The merits of these people will be too abundant to measure and describe."

[*Dāna to Mahāyāna sūtras*[181]]

"Furthermore, Kṣitigarbha! In the future, if there are virtuous men or virtuous women who encounter Mahāyāna sūtras or hear one stanza or one sentence [of the teaching] and they:

     The Sutra of Ksitigarbha's Fundamental Vows

Generate a sincere, respectful mind in praising
as well as
Make offerings and practice dāna with great
reverence,

These persons will gain immense fruitful consequences that are boundless and countless. If they can:

Attribute the blessings to [all beings in] the dharma realms
[instead of claiming the blessings personally],

Such merits thus gained will be too abundant to measure and describe."

[Dāna of Making Restorations]

"Furthermore, Kṣitigarbha! If in the future, there are virtuous men or virtuous women who encounter the Buddhas' stūpas, temples and Mahāyāna sūtras (symbols of the Three Jewels) that are new, and they:

Perform dāna and make offerings,
Behold, pay tribute and admire with praises,
Respectfully join their palms together; and

If they encounter old or damaged ones and:

Make restorations and repairs,
Either solely vow [to take responsibility] or
Persuade many people to join the same vow,

Such people, for the next thirty lifetimes, will always be kings of small nations. The *dānapatis*[182] [who initiate such great tasks] will always [gain the capital to] be wheel-turning kings who will reciprocate with virtuous dharma of the Ten Disciplines, teaching and transforming those kings of small nations."

[Conclusion of Planting Virtuous Roots]

"Therefore, Kṣitigarbha! In the future, if there are virtuous men or virtuous women who:

Plant virtuous roots in the Buddha-dharma, or
Perform dāna and make offerings, or
Repair and restore stūpas and temples, or
Fix and arrange [damaged and neglected] sūtras,

Even if such virtuous deeds are as small as a strand of hair, a mote of dust, a grain of sand or a droplet of water, if they can:

Attribute [the merits] to the dharma realms,

[They are expanding their minds towards the infinite and immeasurable space and time, and] the merits of these people will bring them the enjoyment of superb and exquisite happiness for hundreds of thousands of lifetimes. If they:

Only attribute [the merits] to their close relatives
    [instead of to all beings in the dharma realms] or
Enjoy the benefits personally,

The consequence is that they will enjoy happiness for three lifetimes.

Performing a little [virtuous deed as small as a strand of hair or a droplet of water] will earn ten thousandfold favorable retributions.

     The Sutra of Kṣitigarbha's Fundamental Vows

[What a good investment that is!]"

[Final Conclusion]

"Therefore, O Kṣitigarbha! The [various] causes and conditions [as well as consequences] of performing [different] dāna are thus."

CHAPTER 11:

Protection of the Dharma by God of Solid-Firm-Earth

[Praising the Most Profound Vows of Kṣitigarbha]

At that time, *God of Solid-Firm-Earth* (*Dṛdha-pṛthivī-devatā*)[183] addressed the Buddha: "O Bhagavat, from the remote past, I have been reverently beholding and paying tribute to an infinite number of Bodhisattva Mahāsattvas. All of them [have reached the status of Mahāsattvas because they] have accomplished inconceivable deliverances. With great miraculous power and great wisdom, they have been prevalently and universally rescuing all sentient beings. Nevertheless, only Kṣitigarbha Bodhisattva Mahāsattva, amongst all Bodhisattvas, has made the most profound and solemn of vows.

Bhagavat! This Kṣitigarbha Bodhisattva has great cause-conditions with Jambudvīpa. For example, [the Mahāsattvas] Mañjuśrī, Samantabhadra, *Avalokiteśvara*[184] and Maitreya also [maintain special connections with Jambudvīpa and] transform themselves into hundreds of thousands of identities in the six realms to rescue all sentient beings, and their vows will be realized one day. This Kṣitigarbha Bodhisattva has made His vow to teach and transform all sentient beings in the six realms throughout kalpas as numerous as the sand grains in tens of thousands of billions of Ganges Rivers."

[Benefits of Setting up a Shrine]

"O Bhagavat! I have been observing sentient beings of the present and future. If they:

Find a clean place in the southern location of their
    household; and
With soil, stone, bamboo or wood, make a niche.
In this niche, if they can sculpt or paint—
    even in gold, silver, copper or iron—
    and make an image of Kṣitigarbha,
Burn incense and make offerings,
Gaze upon and pay tribute [to His image], and
Praise and admire [His merits],

By doing so, the sentient beings will immediately gain ten benefits while living in those households. What are the ten benefits?

First, the land [they live on] will be fertile[185].
Second, their households will always be safe and sound[186].
Third, their deceased relatives will be reborn in the
    celestial realm.
Fourth, their living relatives will enjoy longevity.
Fifth, all their wishes will be fulfilled satisfactorily.
Sixth, their households will not encounter any
    misfortune of flood or fire.
Seventh, wastefulness and squandering [of health, wealth
    and blessings] will be eliminated.
Eighth, while asleep, no bad dreams will disturb them.
Ninth, all their comings and goings will be protected
    by gods.
Tenth, they will frequently have the opportunity to
    encounter saintly causes [to make connection with
    the Three Jewels and plant the seed of Bodhi].

O Bhagavat! If all sentient beings of the present and future can make such offerings [to Kṣitigarbha Bodhisattva] in their

 The Sutra of Ksitigarbha's Fundamental Vows

households as instructed above, they will obtain the benefits as listed."

[Promises Made by God of Solid-Firm-Earth]

Again, God of Solid-Firm-Earth said to the Buddha: "O Bhagavat! In the future [Dharma-Declining Period], if there are some virtuous men and virtuous women who can:

> *Place this Sūtra and the image of Kṣitigarbha Bodhisattva*
> *in their households; and further*
> *Read and recite this Sūtra [themselves and for others]; and*
> *Make offerings to this Bodhisattva,*

I will use my miraculous power to protect and bless them day and night. Even those calamities of flood, fire, robbery, theft, major or minor misfortunes and all evil matters will be totally kept out."

[The Buddha's Entrustment]

The Buddha told God of Solid-Firm-Earth: "You possess great miraculous power that is far superior to the powers of other gods. Why? It is because all the land in Jambudvīpa is under your command and protection. All the grass, trees, sand, rocks, rice, hemp, bamboo, reeds, grain, crops and treasures emerge from the earth. Their presence is due to your [great miraculous] power.

Moreover, you have always proclaimed and praised the merits of Kṣitigarbha Bodhisattva about how He benefits all sentient beings. Therefore, your meritorious virtues and miraculous powers are hundreds of thousands of times greater than the powers of other deities.

O God of Earth! In the future [Dharma-Declining Period], if there are virtuous men and virtuous women who:

Make offerings to the Bodhisattva; also
Read and recite this Sūtra;
Cultivate and practice solely according to the teachings
in The Sūtra of Kṣitigarbha's Fundamental Vows,

You shall protect them with your miraculous power. Do not let them hear[187] of all the harmful disasters and unpleasant events, lest the harms reach them. Not only will you be protecting these people, but Lord Śakra, Lord Brahmā and their subordinates, as well as other celestial beings and their subordinates, will also protect them.

Why shall these virtuous men and virtuous women receive protection and blessings from these Bodhisattvas and Sages?

It is all due to the fact that they have been beholding and paying tribute to the image of Kṣitigarbha, as well as reading and reciting this Sūtra of fundamental vows. Naturally at the end, they will be liberated from the Suffering Sea [of perpetual births and deaths] to validate the happiness of nirvāṇa. That is the reason why they will be protected and blessed."

The Benefits of Beholding Kṣitigarbha's Image and Learning His Name

[Resetting the Stage]

At that time, Bhagavat radiated hundreds of thousands of myriads of millions of majestic, fine rays[188] from the crown of His head, namely:

> The fine white rays;
> The brilliant, fine white rays;
> The fine auspicious rays;
> The brilliant, fine auspicious rays;
> The fine jade rays;
> The brilliant, fine jade rays;
> The fine purple rays;
> The brilliant, fine purple rays;
> The fine indigo rays;
> The brilliant, fine indigo rays;
> The fine blue rays;
> The brilliant, fine blue rays;
> The fine rcd rays;
> The brilliant, fine red rays;
> The fine green rays;
> The brilliant, fine green rays;
> The fine golden rays;
> The brilliant, fine golden rays;
> The fine celebration-cloud rays;
> The brilliant, fine celebration-cloud rays;
> The fine thousand-wheel rays;
> The brilliant, fine thousand-wheel rays;
> The fine jeweled-wheel rays;

The brilliant, fine jeweled-wheel rays;
The fine sun-wheel rays;
The brilliant, fine sun-wheel rays;
The fine moon-wheel rays;
The brilliant, fine moon-wheel rays;
The fine palace rays;
The brilliant, fine palace rays;
The fine ocean-cloud rays; and
The brilliant, fine ocean-cloud rays.

[*Giving Admiration*]

After radiating those fine rays from the crown of His head, Bhagavat further transmitted majestic and exquisite voices. He made the following proclamation to all present, including the devas, nāgas and others of the Eight Legions, humans and non-humans:

"Hear me today in the Palace of Trāyastriṃśa Heaven, as I have praised, advocated, acclaimed and exclaimed Kṣitigarbha Bodhisattva's beneficial deeds in the human and celestial realms [in saving others and advancing Himself[189]], deeds that are inconceivable, deeds with superb saintly causes, deeds of realizing the Tenth Stage [on the Path of Bodhisattva] and ultimately, deeds of no regression[190] from attaining Anuttara-samyak-saṃbodhi."

[*Making Requests and the Response*]

As those words were said, among the assembly there was a Bodhisattva Mahāsattva bearing the name Avalokiteśvara, who stood up from His seat, knelt on His right knee, and with palms together reverently addressed the Buddha: "O Bhagavat, this Kṣitigarbha Bodhisattva Mahāsattva has great kindness and mercy. He is most empathetic towards all sinful, suffering and distressed beings.

          The Sutra of Kṣitigarbha's Fundamental Vows

In tens of thousands of millions upon millions of worlds, with all His meritorious virtues and inconceivable, majestic, miraculous power, He transforms Himself into infinite tens of thousands of millions upon millions of divided-identical bodies [to accomplish the tasks of saving others and Himself]. I have heard Bhagavat and the infinite numbers of Buddhas in the ten directions unanimously praise and admire Kṣitigarbha Bodhisattva saying, 'If we asked the presences of all the Buddhas in the past, present and future to speak of His meritorious virtues, such a speech would be endless.'

[Avalokiteśvara continued:] Earlier, I have heard Bhagavat [delightfully and] prevalently proclaiming to all present, wishing to praise Kṣitigarbha's merits of benefitting [and elevating infinite numbers of sentient beings]. Now I solely hope that you, Bhagavat, will speak, for the sake of all present and future sentient beings, of your admiration and praise about Kṣitigarbha's inconceivable work, so those sentient beings will behold and pay tribute to Him and gain blessings."

[Planting the Cause]

The Buddha told Avalokiteśvara Bodhisattva: "You have had special and profound affinities with the Sahā World. If devas, nāgas, men, women, gods, ghosts and even sinful suffering beings in the six realms:

Learn about your name;
See your image;
Admire and long for you;
Exclaim and praise you,

These beings will frequently be reborn in the realms of celestial beings and humans to enjoy superb and exquisite pleasures. For those who have vowed to advance themselves through cultivating the Unsurpassed Path [of Bodhisattva], they will certainly not regress. When the cause-consequence comes to maturity, they will encounter a Buddha to bestow upon them their future destinies [saying, 'You will become a Buddha'].

Since you have great kindness, mercy and empathy towards all sentient beings as well as the devas, nāgas and others of the Eight Legions, I will proclaim and describe the inconceivable accomplishments of Kṣitigarbha Bodhisattva and how He benefits these sentient beings. Listen attentively, I will explain for you now."

Avalokiteśvara said: "Yes, Bhagavat! I am most happy to hear."

[*Rescuing and Benefitting Celestial Beings*]

The Buddha told Avalokiteśvara Bodhisattva: "In the various worlds of the present and future, when the blessings of celestial beings come to an end [and they are on the verge of death], the Five Signs of Decay[191] will appear; perhaps some will fall into the evil realms.

If these celestial beings, regardless whether they are male or female, when these signs appear, would:

See the image of Kṣitigarbha Bodhisattva; or
Learn about the name of Kṣitigarbha Bodhisattva; or
Make an obeisance with each gaze,

The celestial blessings of these celestial beings will be increased so that they can enjoy great happiness, and they will never fall into the three evil realms as retribution. In addition, if they:

    The Sutra of Kṣitigarbha's Fundamental Vows

*Behold the Bodhisattva's image and learn about
    His name, as well as
Give alms and make offerings with incense,
    flowers, clothing, food and drink,
    treasures and jeweled necklaces,*

The merits and benefits thus gained will be infinite and boundless."

[*Rescuing at the Time of Death*]

"Furthermore, Avalokiteśvara! If sentient beings in the six realms, in all the worlds of the present and future, while on the verge of their deaths can:

*Learn about the name of Kṣitigarbha Bodhisattva; and
Let the name register in their ears and minds,*

These beings will never fall into the three evil realms to endure suffering, not to mention if at the time of death, the parents and other dependents can perform some virtuous deeds on this dying person's behalf, namely:

*Donating his property, wealth, treasures and clothing
    in order to sculpt or paint the image of Kṣitigarbha;*

Or, before his death, while he is still able to see and hear,

*Let him know that his dependents have donated all his
    property, treasures and so forth in order to sculpt
    and paint Kṣitigarbha Bodhisattva's image on
    his behalf.*

If this person deserves to suffer the grave illness as karmic retribution, the merits of making the offerings will [save him from his deserved suffering and] enable him to recover from his illness instantly, and his lifespan will be increased.

If this person is destined to die as his karmic retribution, and all his sinful, karmic barriers would have made him fall into the evil realms, because of the merits of the offerings, after his death, he will be reborn in the realms of human or celestial beings to enjoy superb and exquisite pleasures. All his sinful barriers will be completely eradicated."

[Benefits for Those Who Have Lost a Parent or Sibling[192]]
[First benefit—Lost relatives liberated from evil realms]

"Furthermore, Avalokiteśvara Bodhisattva! In the future, there are men or women whose parents, brothers or sisters have passed away, or they have been separated from them when they were infants, or when they were three, five or less than ten years old. If later on, after growing up, they think of their deceased or separated relatives and wonder [among infinite numbers of realms and worlds] which realm and which world they have been reborn into, or if they have been reborn in a celestial realm, these men or women must personally:

> *Sculpt or paint Kṣitigarbha Bodhisattva's image; even*
> *Learn about [and chant] His name; and*
> *Make obeisance with each gaze upon His image for*
>   *one to seven days without regressing from the*
>   *original vows of contemplating [and chanting]*
>   *His name, beholding His image, paying tribute*
>   *and making offerings.*

Their relatives who have fallen into the three evil realms,

because of their own grave evil deeds, are destined to stay there for several kalpas. However, due to the merits of these men, women, brothers and sisters in sculpting, painting and beholding Kṣitigarbha's image, the relatives will immediately be liberated from the three evil paths and be reborn in the human or celestial realms. For those who are enjoying superb and exquisite pleasures, due to the merits [offered by their living dependents], those relatives' connections with the Three Jewels will in turn grow and they will enjoy infinite happiness.

[Second benefit—Seeing Kṣitigarbha Bodhisattva and learning the whereabouts of deceased relatives]

If, for twenty-one days, these men and women with deceased or lost relatives can further:

> *Behold the image of Kṣitigarbha wholeheartedly; and*
> *Chant His name a total of ten thousand times,*

The Bodhisattva will appear to them with His boundless body and tell them which world their deceased relatives are presently in. Or, in their dreams, the Bodhisattva will appear, and with His great miraculous power, lead them to the various worlds to see their deceased relatives.

[Third benefit—Gaining life-long protection and blessings]

If these relatives can further:

> *Chant the Bodhisattva's name one thousand*
> *times each day for one thousand days,*

These persons will be protected and sustained throughout their lives by the ghosts and gods dispatched by the Bodhisattva that are in charge of the land in their vicinity.

Their daily necessities will be abundant without illnesses and suffering; even accidents and calamities will not befall their households, let alone physical harms.

Ultimately, the Bodhisattva will rub the crowns of their heads and bestow upon them their future destinies."

[Advancing with Great Vows]

"Furthermore, Avalokiteśvara Bodhisattva! If, in the future, there are virtuous men or virtuous women who wish:

> To make a grand vow of kindness to rescue and help
>   all beings; or
> To pursue the Unsurpassed Bodhi [so as to become
>   a fully enlightened being—a Buddha]; or
> To leave the [burning] Three Realms[193], and
>   these persons, who:

> *Behold the image of Kṣitigarbha and learn about*
> *   His name,*
> *Wholeheartedly take homage [in the Bodhisattva]; or*
> *With incense, fresh flowers, clothing, treasures,*
> *   food and drink, make offerings, gaze and*
> *   make obeisance [to the image],*

These virtuous men and women will soon have their wishes and vows fulfilled, never encountering any tribulations or obstacles."

[Fulfilling Wishes]

"Furthermore, Avalokiteśvara! If, in the future, there are virtuous

                    The Sutra of Kṣitigarbha's Fundamental Vows

men and virtuous women who wish to fulfill hundreds of thousands of myriads of millions of vows and accomplish hundreds of thousands of myriads of millions of tasks during the present time and future, they should:

Take homage,
Behold and pay tribute,
Make offerings, and
Admire and praise the image of Kṣitigarbha
 Bodhisattva,

Then, all their wishes and requests will be fulfilled. If they further pray:

'May Kṣitigarbha Bodhisattva have great kindness
 and mercy to sustain and protect me forever,'

These persons, in their dreams, will swiftly receive blessings from the Bodhisattva who will touch their heads and bestow upon them their future destinies."

[*Removing Karmic Barriers in Learning sūtras*]

"Furthermore, Avalokiteśvara Bodhisattva! If, in the future, there are virtuous men and virtuous women who:

Treasure and respect Mahāyāna sūtras with great
 profoundness; and
Have initiated an admiring and longing mind to read
 and recite the sūtras;
But even after encountering wise and enlightened mentors
 guiding and encouraging them to be familiar with the
 verses, they soon forget what they have learned; and

Even after years and months of study, they are still
    unable to read and recite,

These virtuous men and women have unresolved karmic
barriers generated in their past lives, thus they are unable to read
and recite the Mahāyāna sūtras. If such people:

Learn about the name of Kṣitigarbha Bodhisattva;
Behold Kṣitigarbha Bodhisattva's image; and
Express their wish with an utmost respectful mind
    [how they admire and treasure the Mahāyāna
    sūtras]; furthermore,
Make offerings to the Bodhisattva with incense,
    fresh flowers, clothing, food and drink
    and all their beloved treasures.
Place a bowl of clean water in front of the Bodhisattva
    for one day and one night; then
Pray with folded palms for His empowerment; and
    while facing south,
Drink the bowl of water sincerely and respectfully, and

After taking the water, for the next seven to twenty-one days:

Refrain from taking the five pungent vegetables[194],
    liquor and meat; also
Avoid sexual misconduct, deceptive speech and killing.

These virtuous men and virtuous women will, while sleeping,
see Kṣitigarbha Bodhisattva manifest His boundless body to pour
blessed water upon their heads. Upon awakening, their mind will
be bright and acute. They will respond well to the sūtras, forever
remember them and never forget even one stanza or one sentence
after hearing them."

    The Sutra of Kṣitigarbha's Fundamental Vows

[*Rescuing the Ill-fated*]

"Furthermore, Avalokiteśvara Bodhisattva! If, in the future, there are people:

> Who lack food and clothing; or
> Whose wishes are unfulfilled; or
> Who are frequently distressed by illnesses; or
> Who have encountered many tragedies; or
> Whose households are in constant turmoil, with
>   relatives either scattered or passed away; or
> Who frequently encounter unexpected misfortunes
>   and accidents; or
> Who, even in sleep, are troubled by frightening and
>   horrific nightmares, and these people:

> *Learn about Kṣitigarbha's name;*
> *Behold Kṣitigarbha's image;*
> *Pay respect wholeheartedly; and*
> *Chant [His name] ten thousand times,*

All these unfortunate matters will recede gradually, disappearing entirely. They will promptly have blissful peace and happiness, plentiful food and clothing and even, while sleeping, serenity and contentment."

[*Safety for Travelers*]

"Furthermore, Avalokiteśvara Bodhisattva! If, in the future, there are virtuous men and virtuous women who need to travel:

> Either to make a living; or
> For personal or business reasons; or

Because they are threatened by life and
  death issues; or
For emergency matters,

They may need to enter mountains and wilderness, cross rivers and oceans, or pass treacherous paths where accidents and dangers are common. Before taking the trip, they should:

*Chant Kṣitigarbha Bodhisattva's name ten
  thousand times,*

So that the ghosts and gods along the way will protect and sustain them. They will always have safety and happiness while walking, resting, sitting and sleeping. Even if they encounter tigers, wolves, lions and all other dangerous and poisonous creatures, they will not be harmed."

[*Entrustment*]

The Buddha told Avalokiteśvara Bodhisattva: "This Kṣitigarbha Bodhisattva has the most intimate relationship with sentient beings in Jambudvīpa. If I were to describe the details of how He benefits and uplifts those sentient beings who behold His image and learn about [and respectfully chant] His name [or honor Him in many other ways], I would not be able to do so even by taking hundreds of thousands of kalpas of time.

Therefore, Avalokiteśvara, you must apply your miraculous power to circulate this Sūtra so that sentient beings in the Saha World can forever enjoy blissful peace and happiness for hundreds of thousands of millions of kalpas."

     The Sutra of Ksitigarbha's Fundamental Vows

[*Concluding Stanza*]

"Then, Bhagavat spoke the following stanza:

As I examine Kṣitigarbha's miraculous power,
Kalpas as numerous as sand grains in the Ganges River
     is hardly enough time to speak of them all.
Beholding [His image], learning [His name], gazing and
     paying tribute for a split moment,
Benefits humans and celestial beings in infinite ways.

Any men or women or nāgas and gods,
When their blessings are exhausted, shall fall into the
     evil realms.
Intently pay homage to the [boundless] body of this
     Mahāsattva,
Their longevity will increase and sinful barriers removed.

Those who lost their beloved parents when young,
Not knowing in which realm they have reincarnated.
Brothers, sisters as well as relatives,
From birth to growing up, had no chance to know
     them.
Either sculpt or paint this Mahāsattva's image,
Admiringly with grief, gaze and pay tribute without
     distraction, and
Chant His name for a full three weeks,
The Bodhisattva will appear with the boundless body, and
Show them in which realms the relatives are reborn,
Even if fallen into evil paths, liberation will be swift.
If they could advance without retreating from initial vows,
The crowns of their heads will be touched for saintly
     destiny.

Those who desire to cultivate the Unsurpassed Bodhi,
Even to leave the sufferings of the Three Realms,
As they make the vow of grand kindness,
Should first behold and pay tribute to the Mahāsattva's image.
All their wishes will soon be realized, and
No karmic barriers can ever hinder and block them.

Those who pledge to learn the sūtras, and
Wish to help lost beings reach the other shore,
Although such vows are inconceivable,
They forget soon after learning, all efforts in vain.
These people, obstructed and deluded by karma,
Thus cannot memorize the Mahāyāna sūtras.
Make offerings to Kṣitigarbha with incense, flowers,
Clothing, food, drink and pleasurable things;
Place [a bowl of] clean water in front of the Mahāsattva,
After one day and one night, pray before drinking it;
With a sincere, profound mind, refrain from the five
    pungent greens,
Alcohol, meat, sexual misconduct and deceptive speech.
For twenty-one days, do not kill,
Intently contemplate and chant the Mahāsattva's name.
Promptly, while asleep, they will see His boundless body,
Upon awakening, sensory roots become acute.
Once they hear the teachings of the sūtras,
For tens of millions of lives, they will never forget.
Because this Mahāsattva is so inconceivable,
He can endow these people with such wisdom.

Sentient beings in poverty and illness,
Households in distress and relatives separated,
With troubled sleep and disturbed dreams,
Wishes unfulfilled and prayers not granted.

   The Sutra of Kṣitigarbha's Fundamental Vows

Intently behold and pay tribute to Kṣitigarbha's image,
All evil matters will totally disappear,
Finally all dreams will be at peace, with
Plentiful food and clothing, protection by gods and ghosts.

Those who wish to pass mountains, forests and oceans,
Where poisonous, wicked birds, beasts and evil people,
Vicious gods, ghosts and malicious winds await,
All these hardships and troubles lay ahead.
Should one behold [His image], pay tribute, make offerings,
Chant this Mahāsattva's name ten thousand times,
Then in mountains, forests and oceans,
All evils will thus disappear.

Avalokiteśvara, listen attentively to what I say!
Kṣitigarbha's infinite merits are inconceivable,
Even hundreds of thousands of millions of kalpas is not
    enough to speak of them.
Let the powers of the Mahāsattva be widely known.

If people learn about Kṣitigarbha's name,
Even behold His image with reverence,
Offer incense, flowers, clothing, food and drink—
Hundreds of thousands of dāna—will enjoy blessings
    and exquisite happiness.
If one can attribute these [merits] to the dharma realms,
Eventually one surpasses the cycle of birth-and-death,
    achieving Buddhahood.

Therefore, Avalokiteśvara, you must understand [all of
    the above, and]
Prevalently announce to all the worlds, as numerous
    as the sand grains in the Ganges River.

CHAPTER 13:

Entrustment of Humans and Celestial Beings

[*Entrustment*]

At that time, Bhagavat raised His golden-hued arm, and again, touched the crown of Kṣitigarbha Bodhisattva Mahāsattva's head, saying: "Kṣitigarbha! Kṣitigarbha! Your miraculous power is inconceivable, your kindness and mercy is inconceivable, your wisdom is inconceivable and your eloquence is inconceivable. If all the Buddhas from the ten directions were to praise and proclaim your inconceivable feats, they could not finish even in tens of millions of kalpas.

O Kṣitigarbha! Kṣitigarbha! Remember today at Trāyastriṃśa Heaven, in this great assembly of hundreds of thousands of myriads of millions of unspeakable-unspeakable attendants, including all the Buddhas, Bodhisattvas as well as the devas, nāgas and others of the Eight Legions, I am once more entrusting you to safeguard all human and celestial beings and those who are unable to leave the Burning Three Realms. Do not let these sentient beings fall into the evil realms, not even for one day and one night, lest they fall into the Five Unremitting Hells and Avīci Hell to experience sufferings that will last for tens of thousands of millions upon millions of kalpas, with no chance to escape. [Do not let sentient beings of the present and future go through that kind of suffering again.]

O Kṣitigarbha! These sentient beings of southern Jambudvīpa, their inclinations and vows sway due to their uncertainty [which is caused by their habitual karmic forces], and it pushes them to lean towards evils incessantly. Even if they have generated some benevolent mind and thoughts, a moment later they will regress from that virtue again. When encountering unfavorable conditions, their minds [will lean towards evil, and that is the time the evil thoughts] will grow and expand continuously. For these reasons, I divide myself into tens of thousands of billions of transformed bodies to educate and rescue them. [Regardless how little their virtuous roots are in response to enlightenment,] I will elicit their virtuous roots according to their current situation so they can gain salvation and liberation."

[Entrusting Celestial Beings and Humans]

"O Kṣitigarbha! Today, I earnestly entrust to you these celestial beings and humans: In the future, if there are celestial beings or virtuous men and virtuous women who plant a few virtuous roots [of faith, of vigilance, of contemplative thinking, of Samādhi or of wisdom] according to the Buddha-dharma, even if these virtuous roots are as small as a strand of hair, a mote of dust, a grain of sand or a droplet of water, you will apply your miraculous power to swiftly rescue them and protect them. Be sure that they will [make the vows to] cultivate the Unsurpassed Bodhi according to the stages. Do not let them get lost [on the path, thus forgetting their original vows] and regrettably regress."

[Entrusting those at the Threshold of Evil Realms]

"Furthermore, Kṣitigarbha! In the future, if any celestial beings and humans, driven by their karmic forces, are about to fall into the three evil realms, at the moment of falling or having reached the threshold of the three evil realms, if these sentient beings think of one Buddha's name, or one Bodhisattva's name, or one sentence or one stanza from a Mahāyāna sūtra, I am asking you to rescue them with all your miraculous and convenient powers. Please appear in front of them with your boundless body and shatter their hells. Let

   The Sutra of Ksitigarbha's Fundamental Vows

them be reborn in heaven so as to enjoy supreme happiness."

Then, Bhagavat stated the following stanza:

"Those celestial beings and humans of the
        present and future,
        I eagerly entrust them to you—
    Save them with your great miraculous
        power and conveniences,
        Do not let them fall into those evil paths."

[*The Promise*]

At that time, Kṣitigarbha Bodhisattva Mahāsattva, kneeled on His right knee and with folded palms, He addressed the Buddha, "O Bhagavat, I solely wish that you, Bhagavat, will not worry about this anymore. In the future, as long as there are virtuous men and virtuous women who:

> *Generate a respectful mind towards the Three Jewels,*
>   *even for a split moment,*

I will also exert hundreds of thousands of convenient ways to swiftly rescue and liberate them from birth and death; let alone those who have always made efforts to learn the authentic dharma and follow the teachings with faithful practice. I will make sure that on the Unsurpassed Path, they will never regress."

[*The Benefits*]

As these words were said, a Bodhisattva in the assembly named *Space Treasury* (*Ākāśagarbha*)[195] said to the Buddha, "O Bhagavat! After arriving in Trāyastriṃśa, I have heard you, Tathāgata, admire and praise Kṣitigarbha Bodhisattva for His inconceivable, majestic, miraculous powers. In the future, if there are virtuous men and virtuous women, or celestial beings and nāgas, who learn about this Sūtra and [chant and praise] the name of Kṣitigarbha, as well as behold His image with respect, how many benefits will they receive? [And what are the benefits?] I wholeheartedly wish that you, Bhagavat, will give a general explanation for sentient beings of the present and future."

[Benefits for Virtuous Men and Women]

The Buddha told Space Treasury Bodhisattva, "Listen attentively! Listen attentively! I am going to explain [the benefits] for you one by one. If in the future, there are virtuous men or virtuous women who:

> *Behold the image of Kṣitigarbha, and*
> *Learn about this Sūtra, even read it aloud,*
> *Perform dāna and make offerings with incense, fresh*
>   *flowers, food and drink, clothing and treasures,*
> *Praise, admire, behold and pay tribute [to the image*
>   *of this Bodhisattva and His merits],*

They will obtain the following twenty-eight benefits:

First, they will be protected and cared for by devas and nāgas
     [as well as ghosts and gods].
Second, [because of their virtuous deeds] the virtuous fruit
     they receive will increase daily.
Third, they will accumulate superb causes [to pursue the
     Unsurpassed Bodhi].
Fourth, their vows of pursuing the Bodhi will not regress.
Fifth, all their daily necessities—food and clothing—will be
     abundant.

     The Sutra of Kṣitigarbha's Fundamental Vows

Sixth, they will not be infected by illness or contagious disease.
Seventh, calamities of flood and fire will keep a distance
    from them.
Eighth, they will not encounter any robbers nor thieves.
Ninth, they will be respected and admired by those who
    see them.
Tenth, they will be guarded and assisted by gods and ghosts.
Eleventh, if born as women [in this lifetime], they can be
    reborn as men [in their future lifetimes, leaving the
    sufferings of womanhood behind].
Twelfth, [if they wish to continue to be born as women in
    their future lives,] they will be born in noble families as
    daughters of high officers or kings.
Thirteenth, they will have fine physical features and good
    characters.
Fourteenth, they will often be born in various heavens.
Fifteenth, they may be [reborn as mundane leaders such as]
    emperors or kings [or wheel-turning kings or Lord Śakras].
Sixteenth, they will have knowledge about their past lives.
Seventeenth, all their wishes and vows will be satisfactorily
    answered.
Eighteenth, all their relatives and dependants will live in
    blissful happiness.
Nineteenth, all misfortunes and accidents will disappear from
    their lives.
Twentieth, they will never fall into the karmic reincarnations
    [among the six realms of existence].
Twenty-first, [not only will their future whereabouts be
    blissful,] they will have the miraculous power to go
    anywhere they wish without hindrance.
Twenty-second, they will sleep well with pleasant dreams.
Twenty-third, all their deceased relatives will depart from
    sufferings [of the three evil realms].

Twenty-fourth, they will be reborn based on past merits.
Twenty-fifth, because of their virtuous merits, they will be
    praised and hailed by the Buddhas and Bodhisattvas.
Twenty-sixth, they will be alert and bright; their six sensory
    roots [—the eyes, ears, nose, tongue, body and mind—]
    will be harmonious and acute.
Twenty-seventh, they will have minds of great kindness
    and mercy.
Twenty-eighth, they will eventually become Buddhas."

[*Benefits for Celestial Beings, Nāgas, Ghosts and Gods*]

[The Buddha continued,] "Furthermore, O Space Treasury Bodhisattva! If celestial beings, nāgas, ghosts and gods of the present and
future:

Learn the name of Kṣitigarbha; and
Pay tribute to Kṣitigarbha's image; or
Learn about how Kṣitigarbha carried out His
    great fundamental vows with virtuous deeds; and
Admire, praise, behold and make obeisance,

They will gain the following seven benefits:

First, [while cultivating the Bodhi paths] they will swiftly
    pass through the saintly stages[196].
Second, their evil karmic deeds [of past innumerable kalpas]
    will be eradicated.
Third, they will always be protected and cared for by
    many Buddhas.
Fourth, their vows of pursuing the Bodhi will not regress.
Fifth, the power derived from their vows will increase
    continuously.

     The Sutra of Kṣitigarbha's Fundamental Vows

Sixth, they will have great, miraculous wisdom of
    knowing their past lives.
Seventh, they will ultimately become Buddhas."

[*Final Tributes*]

At that time from the ten directions, unspeakable-unspeakable
numbers of Buddha-Tathāgatas as well as Mahāsattvas, the devas,
nāgas and others of the Eight Legions—who heard how Śākyamuni
Buddha praised and admired the great miraculous power of
Kṣitigarbha Bodhisattva as being inconceivable—[unanimously]
exclaimed: This is unprecedented!

Then, Trāyastrimśa Heaven rained innumerable amounts of
incense, flowers, celestial garments, pearls and necklaces as offerings
to Śākyamuni Buddha and Kṣitigarbha Bodhisattva. After the
offering, all the assembly members beheld and paid obeisance [to
both of them], and with palms together, they withdrew.

Kṣitigarbha's Gāthā

Alas! We suffering beings of this Dharma-Declining Period,
Gravely entangling with sin, we fall into the murky realms.
The three poison fires of the mind
bring forth harsh misfortunes;
The seven deeds of action and speech
offend ghosts and gods.
Reincarnating repeatedly on the karmic path
is not His wish.
Drifting in and out of the evil paths
contradicts His grace.
Who will rescue us out of the endless sufferings?
The kindness and mercy of Kṣitigarbha,
with His solemn vows will!

In Praise of Kṣitigarbha

The supreme enlightenment of the Bodhi
radiates with kindness and mercy!
Your profound grand vows
bear and shoulder all!
Beings from the ten directions
arrive at Trāyastriṃśa Heaven.
The illumination penetrates Avīci Hell.
While gazing upon and saluting the holy images,
I repent and entrust all my mundane sins.

*Composed in rhythmic Chinese by the late
Master Sheng Chang Hwang*

Endnotes

Chapter 1

1 *Dharma* is a Sanskrit word from ancient India meaning "any thing or phenomenon such as an event, attribute, being or existence" and in Buddhism, refers to the teachings of the Buddha on the absolute truth, virtue, law, causes and consequences. It is about how everything, including sentient beings, comes into being (into the visible world) and disappears again (into the invisible world). In the mundane world, any law, rule, regulation, guideline or "entity" is also considered a dharma.

2 *Trāyastrimśa* Heaven, also called the Thirty-Three Heavens, is situated on the top of Mount Sumeru and is the 2nd level of the six heavens of the Realm of Desire. Lady *Māyā*, the Buddha's mundane mother who passed away seven days after giving birth to Prince *Siddhārtha*, was reincarnated in Trāyastrimśa Heaven. Prince Siddhārtha later became Śākyamuni Buddha. See *Sahā World* map.

3 Lady *Māyā* was the Buddha Śākyamuni's mundane birth mother. *Māyā* in Sanskrit means "illusion". Lady Māyā giving birth to Prince Siddhārtha, who later became a Buddha, was a manifestation—the truth is that Śākyamuni was already fully enlightened long before He was born to Lady Māyā. He knew how to bring together all the necessary elements in order to appear in this visible world, and He also knew how to disintegrate these elements so as to fade into the invisible world. Therefore, by being born, He was only complying with the "rules" of this mundane world.

4 Inexpressible was one of the numerical units used in ancient India. Terms, from small to large, such as *nayuta*, *asamkhyeya*, inexpressible and inexpressible-inexpressible, are commonly seen in Buddhist sūtras. See *numerical units* in Glossary.

5 *Bodhisattva* is a Sanskrit word meaning "enlightened being". *Bodhi* is "enlightenment" and *sattva* is "sentient being". Bodhisattvas are enlightened beings who work on the mutual cultivation towards enlightenment of all beings.

6 *Mahāsattva* is Sanskrit for a "great being". *Mahā* means "great" and *sattva* means "sentient being". When a sentient being has reached

the 6th stage on the Path of Bodhisattva, the designation *Bodhisattva Mahāsattva* (or only Mahāsattva by itself) is used. There are ten stages on the Path before a bodhisattva validates the status of a Buddha.

7   The ten directions refer to the ten directions of space, i.e. the eight points of the compass—north, south, east, west, northeast, northwest, southeast, southwest—plus zenith (up) and nadir (down). Figuratively means "all directions" or "everywhere".

8   *Śākyamuni* (or *Shakyamuni*) is the name of the Buddha who appeared in this civilization. In Sanskrit, *śākya* means "able, possible, practicable or capable" and is the name of His clan; *muni* means "sage". The word *Buddha* means "Enlightened One". Therefore, anyone who pursues the path of enlightenment by following Śākyamuni's teachings and footsteps can become a Buddha.

9   Evil times refers to the Dharma-Declining Period in the Sahā World, the physical world that we are currently in, where sentient beings' minds are dark, suffering is most severe and the world is filled with contention and disasters.

10   The Five Contaminations of the Sahā World explain why sentient beings of this time and place suffer so prevalently. They are: 1. *Contamination of Kalpa*, the era we are in is contaminated, a troubled and chaotic time when no one is spared; 2. *Contamination of Views*, our views are contaminated, as we are unable to correctly cognize and understand ourself nor our objective reality; 3. *Contamination of Afflictions*, our worldly cares, desires and state of mind are contaminated, misdirected by our evil deeds (greed, hatred, arrogance), thus constantly engaging in contention, creating confusion, distress and suffering; 4. *Contaminated Beings*, we are obstinate, hard-to-tame, habitual evildoing, sinful, suffering beings, thus creating barriers to enlightenment; and 5. *Contaminated Destiny*, because of the previous four characteristics, we lack a higher mission and a meaningful goal in life, which also results in a short lifespan.

11   Sentient being is *sattva* in Sanskrit and refers to living beings with feeling and sentiment who perceive and respond with existing sensory roots, such as humans with their six roots of eyes, ears, nose, tongue, body and mind. There are six realms of sentient beings—celestial beings, humans, asuras, hungry ghosts, animals and hell beings. Each sentient being is born into one of these realms according to the virtuous or evil deeds that one has committed.

    The Sutra of Ksitigarbha's Fundamental Vows

12 "Law" is *dharma* in Buddhism. The *Law of Suffering and Happiness* has two points of importance. First is to know the true meaning of suffering (impotence about the Eight Sufferings) and happiness (departing from one's ten evils) as taught by the Buddha. Second is that only after learning about the Truth of Suffering (First Noble Truth), can one have the momentum to seek true happiness.

13 *Bhagavat* in Sanskrit means "holy, venerable and revered". It is one of the ten designations of the Buddha. See *Bhagavat* in Glossary.

14 *Tathāgata*, an honorable designation of a Buddha, means "one who has come from the realm of truth", indicating a fully enlightened being who embodies the fundamental truth of all transitory phenomena and has grasped the law of causality spanning past, present and future. *Tathāgata* also means "thus come one" which indicates one who has arrived from the realm of truth or "thus gone one", indicating one who has gone to the world of enlightenment. Here, it refers to Śākyamuni Buddha.

15 *Prajñā* in Sanskrit means "wisdom" or "understanding". It refers to rising above the distinctions of "I" or one's ego to relinquish mundane, dualistic views—dwelling on two extreme ends, such as good or bad, large or small, existent or non-existent—and thus realizing the equal and universal wisdom in regards to all people, events and matters. *Prajñā* is realized through advanced cultivation of the Buddha-dharma. See *Six Pāramitās* in Glossary.

16 *Samādhi* is Sanskrit for "concentration". It is a profound Buddhist meditation aiming to tame the roots of the six senses (eyes, ears, nose, tongue, body and mind)—especially our mind—thus eliciting great wisdom and the blessing to be able to perform miracles.

17 Homage means to pay respect to, take refuge in, entrust to and be guided by the Buddha or Bodhisattvas to be led to ultimate enlightenment as well as to be blessed, protected and empowered by them. See both *homage* and *take homage in the Buddha* in Glossary.

18 *Dāna* is Sanskrit for "almsgiving", "letting go" or "forsaking". There are three kinds of dāna—*dāna of alms* refers to monetary donation; *dāna of service* refers to personally getting involved in worthy causes and being of service; *dāna of dharma* refers to studying, practicing and validating the teachings of the Buddha while helping others to do the same. Each kind of dāna brings different levels of benefits.

In Buddhist cultivation, *dāna* is often paired with another word, *pāramitā*. *Pāramitā* means to "reach the other shore", referring to the shore of ultimate deliverance. Cultivating *Dāna Pāramitā* or any other pāramitā alone will allow the practitioner to attain deliverance. See *Six Pāramitās* in Glossary.

19   *Pāramitā* means "that which has gone beyond" or "to reach the other shore". Often translated as "perfection", it refers to reaching the shore of ultimate deliverance from the shore of suffering by sequentially cultivating each pāramitā while simultaneously cultivating the other nine pāramitās. The ten pāramitās, also called the ten Conveniences of Tathāgata, are the ten stages on the Path of Bodhisattva—*dāna* (forsaking), *śīla* (observing disciplines), *kṣānti* (expanding endurance capacity of the mind), *vīrya* (diligently striving forward), *dhyāna* (mindful abstract contemplation), *prajñā* (wisdom of relinquishing dualistic views), *upāya* (expedient means), *praṇidhāna* (vow, profound meditation), *bala* (strength) and *jñāna* (strength of superb wisdom). The strength of the first *Six Pāramitās* can tame the roots of the six senses and such cultivation will carry a practitioner or a bodhisattva through various stages to the ultimate shore of liberation.

20   *Śīla* in Sanskrit means "virtue, nature, conduct and well-behaved" and refers to observing the disciplines (precepts) defined by the Buddha, such as the Ten Virtuous Disciplines. See *Six Pāramitās* in Glossary.

21   *Kṣānti* in Sanskrit means "receptivity, patience, forbearance or endurance" and refers to expanding one's mind capacity through above-mentioned practices. See *Six Pāramitās* in Glossary.

22   *Vīrya* in Sanskrit means "vigor" or "strength" and refers to advancing diligently and courageously in pursuing deliverance. See *Six Pāramitās* in Glossary.

23   *Dhyāna* in Sanskrit means "contemplation, absorption, abstract meditation, reflection" and refers to conducting mindful focused-penetrating contemplation to halt all major and minor evils as well as to cease all doubts towards the Three Jewels and the Ten Virtuous Disciplines. See *Six Pāramitās* in Glossary.

24   No-outflow (*an-āśrava*) is a mental state or wisdom of being away from the three poison fires of the mind (greed/stinginess, hatred/jealousy and arrogance with erroneous views), achieved through

                    The Sutra of Ksitigarbha's Fundamental Vows

cultivation where one's action, speech and thought no longer bear any harmful effects that would cause a loss or leakage of blessings, virtues and merits.

25   Lion's roar (*siṃhanāda*) denotes leadership, might and fearlessness.

26   *Dharma-voices* are the sound of Truth, referring to miraculous merits of the Buddha who can transmit the dharma through "sound" which can only be perceived by the mind. They carry the teachings of profound dharma, mainly expounded by the Buddha or Bodhisattvas.

27   *Deva*: Sanskrit word for heavenly or celestial being. See *Eight Legions* in Glossary.

28   *Nāga*: Sanskrit word for dragon. See *Eight Legions* in Glossary.

29   *Sahā* World. The Sanskrit word *sahā* means "enduring", "bearing" and "suffering". The physical world we are currently in is called Sahā World because sentient beings are muddle-minded and insensitive to suffering; thus, we are indifferent to seeking true deliverance, even though the world is filled with disasters and pain. However, it is also the best place and best time to achieve swift deliverance once people recognize the Three Jewels and learn the Buddha-dharma.

30   *Dharma-clouds* refer to the miraculous merits of the Buddha who can transmit His dharma through "clouds" which can only be perceived by the mind. These clouds can universally cover and shield all sentient beings, provide peace and refuge, and illuminate our minds with wisdom.

31   *Trāyastriṃśa* Palace is a palace within Trāyastriṃśa Heaven.

32   The heavens refer to the celestial (*deva*) realm or path, one of the six paths in the Sahā World. This path is composed of three realms and 28 heavens: *Realm of Desire* (6 heavens), *Realm of Form* (18 heavens) and *Realm of Formlessness* (4 heavens). In Ch. 1 of this sūtra, 26 heavens are mentioned. See *Sahā World* map.

33   *Mañjuśrī* is considered the guardian of the Buddha-dharma, known for his keen prajñā wisdom. *Mañjuśrī* in Sanskrit means "gentle" or "sweet glory". It is said that all the Buddhas of the past, present and future derive their enlightenment from Him as their mentor. *Mañjuśrī* and *Samantabhadra* are the two Mahāsattvas often depicted on either side of Śākyamuni Buddha.

34   *Kalpa* is a Sanskrit word that refers to an immense measurement of time in ancient India. A small kalpa is represented as 16.8 billion years, and a mahā-kalpa as 1.3 trillion years. Within each kalpa, one thousand Buddhas make their presence known in the Sahā World.

35   *Kṣitigarbha* is a Sanskrit word meaning "earth treasury" or "earth store", which includes the underground treasures and all growths and establishments above the ground; it also reflects the hidden treasures in the minds of all sentient beings. *Kṣiti* means "earth" and *garbha* means "womb". This Mahāsattva is most distinguished for His grand vow to not become a Buddha until all beings, including those in hell, are rescued and transformed. He is the best role model for all Mahāyāna Buddhist practitioners as He demonstrates the importance and indispensability of making grand vows which guide His course, generate His strength and accomplish His deeds of rescuing all beings. He can transform Himself to appear like a mirror image of the being that He is to rescue; He can also create infinite divided-identical bodies so as to rescue infinite sentient beings.

36   Already delivered and transformed refers to the current Buddhas and bodhisattva mahāsattvas from the Buddha lands in the ten directions.

37   To be delivered and transformed refers to arhats, pratyeka-buddhas and the devas, nāgas and others of the Eight Legions.

38   Yet to be delivered and transformed refers to the ghosts from all the Buddha lands in the ten directions.

39   Virtuous Roots refer to the Five Virtuous Roots of faith, diligent advancement, focused thought (on dharma), samādhi (Buddhist meditation) and wisdom. Once the roots are set in fertile soil (mind), they will grow and give strength of faith, strength of diligent advancement, strength of focused thought, strength of samādhi (meditation to elicit wisdom) and strength of wisdom.

40   Four Unhindered Wisdoms are: 1. unhindered wisdom of knowing all profound dharma; 2. unhindered wisdom of understanding the infinite meaning of all dharma; 3. unhindered wisdom of mastering different languages and forms of expression to aptly expound the dharma; and 4. unhindered wisdom of joyfully and tirelessly advocating the dharma according to one's readiness or request.

    The Sutra of Kṣitigarbha's Fundamental Vows

41   *Śrāvaka* is Sanskrit for "one who listens" or "one who is hearing or listening to" and refers to a Small Vehicle (Hīnayāna) practitioner. Also known as a Hearer. See *Hīnayāna* in Glossary.

42   *Hīnayāna*. In Sanskrit, *hīna* means "lesser" or "inferior" and *yāna* means "vehicle"; in Buddhism, it refers to the Small Vehicle. It is one of the three cultivation methods in Buddhism. Small Vehicle practitioners are called Hearers or Śrāvakas, as they hear the dharma directly from the Buddha. The ultimate goal of Hīnayāna is to reach individual emancipation to become an Arhat.

43   "The devas, nagas and others of the Eight Legions" is also known as the Eight Legions. They are: 1. *deva*, celestial being; 2. *nāga*, dragon; 3. *yakṣa*, malignant flesh devourer; 4. *gandharva*, ghost of fragrance and music; 5. *asura*, a contentious being often waging wars with Lord Śakra and his followers; 6. *garuḍa*, king of birds with golden wings who prays on old or sick dragons; 7. *kinnara*, mythical being of song and dance; and 8. *mahoraga*, boa-shaped demon. As minor gods and ghosts, their ultimate duty is to protect the Buddha-dharma and encourage Buddhist practitioners to advance on their path even though, at times, they have to appear vicious.

44   Deeds is *karma* in Sanskrit. In Buddhism, there are three categories of deeds: 1. body/action, 2. mouth/speech and 3. mind/thought. Only a deed that is free of greed/stinginess, hatred/jealousy and arrogance with erroneous views (the deeds of the mind) is without karmic effect. See *virtuous and evil deeds* in Glossary.

45   Cause-stage refers to the time when a seed or cause was planted so as to receive desired results later.

46   "Three thousandfold great cosmic worlds" is a great universe of a billion small worlds; also known as the three thousandfold world system, trichiliocosm or *tri-sāhasra mahā-sāhasraloka-dhātu*. Each trichiliocosm is a Buddha land, such as the Sahā World, where a Buddha appears and guides beings to liberation. See *three thousandfold great cosmic worlds* in Glossary.

47   Realm (or path) refers to the state of existence of a certain category of beings. There are altogether ten realms: Buddhas, bodhisattvas, pratyeka-buddhas, arhats, celestial beings (devas), asuras (which can appear in the celestial realm or in any of the following four realms), humans, hungry ghosts, animals and hell beings.

48   A Hearer is a Small Vehicle (Hīnayāna) practitioner. Also known as a
      Śrāvaka. See *Hīnayāna* in Glossary.

49   A *Pratyeka-buddha* is a cause-awakened and self-realized practitioner
      of the Middle Vehicle (*Madhyamayāna*) whose goal is to validate
      and break through the sequences of the "Twelve Links of Dependent
      Origination—Leading to Existence" revealing how everything, in-
      cluding all sentient beings, comes into existence and eventually goes
      into non-existence. See *Three Vehicles* in Glossary.

50   Virtuous men or virtuous women are those who observe and uphold
      the Ten Virtuous Disciplines.

51   Chanting the name of a *Buddha* or a *Bodhisattva* is a practice that
      brings infinite benefits. 1. Because the names represent their merits,
      contemplating their names will take our mind away from evil thoughts
      and bring us closer to virtue. 2. Chanting is a form of communication
      to make us closely connected with a Buddha or Bodhisattva. 3. Once
      we have formed a good habit of frequent chanting and contemplation
      of the name of a Buddha or Bodhisattva, when we run into a desperate
      situation, we can call out His name like a reflex to be swiftly rescued.
      4. At the time of death when most sentient beings are in pain, agony,
      confusion and shock, the good habit of chanting will help the person
      receive salvation, guidance and protection, so the path of rebirth can
      be guided and uplifted.

52   Thirty-Three Heavens is also known as Trāyastriṃśa Heaven.

53   Evil paths, evil realms or the lower three realms refer to existence as
      hungry ghosts, animals or hell beings. See *Sahā World* map.

54   Six paths (realms) are the paths of hell beings, animals, hungry ghosts,
      humans, celestial beings and asuras who are very contentious in nature
      and spread among the other five paths. Therefore, it is sometimes
      referred to as the "five paths".

55   *Nayuta* in Sanskrit means "myriad" and refers to a very large number.
      Some sources define as 100 billion, others as 100 million or 10 million.
      See *numerical units* in Glossary.

56   *Asaṃkhyeya* is Sanskrit for "innumerable". See *numerical units* in
      Glossary.

57   Dharma-Resemblance Period is the second of four periods that
      describe our relationship with the Three Jewels (Buddha, Dharma,

                                      The Sutra of Kṣitigarbha's Fundamental Vows

Saṃgha). The four periods are: Authentic-Dharma, Dharma-Resemblance, Dharma-Declining and Dharma-Extinction. See *Four Dharma Periods* in Glossary.

58 *Brahman* was the highest and most respected social caste in ancient India, superior to the political and military leaders. Their main responsibilities were to make communications with the invisible world and give advice to the *kṣatriyas*.

59 Virtuous and evil deeds. In Buddhism, the definition of *virtuous* is "beneficial with no harm"; the definition of *evil* is "harmful without benefit". There are ten evil deeds in three categories:

1. three deeds of *body/action*—killing, stealing, sexual misconduct;

2. four deeds of *mouth/speech*—deceptive speech (lying), alienating speech, ill-intended (harmful) speech, frivolous speech;

3. three deeds of *mind/thought*—greed/stinginess, hatred/jealousy, arrogance with erroneous views.

What are virtuous deeds? Departing from these ten evil deeds is doing and practicing virtuous deeds. See *Ten Virtuous Disciplines* in Glossary.

60 Unremitting Hell (or *Avīci* Hell) is the lowest level of the hell realm with the most extreme suffering and most difficult to get out of. Sentient beings who have committed the most grave evil deeds are born here. Details are described in Ch. 3 of this sūtra.

61 The Law (*Dharma*) of Cause and Consequence is also known as the law of causality—the universal law of how all phenomena interrelate and come into being. It consists of four stages: cause, condition, consequence and retribution. See *Dharma (Law) of Cause and Consequence* in Glossary.

62 *Stūpa* in Sanskrit literally means "heap", referring to a burial mound containing the ashes or relics of an enlightened being. In Asia, a stūpa is often referred to as a pagoda.

63 *Yakṣa* is a malignant and violent being, a devourer (of human flesh) who dwells in the earth, air and the lower heavens. See *Eight Legions* in Glossary.

64 *Mahā-cakravāḍa* is the Sanskrit word for Great Iron-Enclosed Mountains, an immense circular mountain wall that surrounds the four great continents and great salty oceans; also where all hells are located. See *Hells & Karmic Seas* map.

65 *Jambudvīpa* is the name of the continent we inhabit. Because it is situated south of Mount Sumeru, it is also called Southern Jambu-dvīpa. *Jambu* is the name of a tree said to abound in Jambudvīpa, thus its name. See *Sahā World* map.

66 Evil deeds refer to the Ten Evil Deeds which cause harmful, harsh consequences. They are: killing, stealing and sexual misconduct (3 body/action deeds); deceptive speech (lying), alienating speech, ill-intended (harmful) speech and frivolous speech (4 mouth/speech deeds); greed/stinginess, hatred/jealousy and arrogance with erroneous views (3 mind/thought deeds). Refer to *The Sūtra of the Path of Ten Virtuous Deeds*. See also *Ten Virtuous Disciplines* in Glossary.

67 See Ch. 7 for detailed instructions on what to do for newly deceased.

68 *Yojana* is an ancient Indian measure of distance. One *yojana* is about 10 kilometers or 6 miles.

69 *Avīci* Hell (or Unremitting Hell). The lowest level of the hell realm with the most extreme suffering and most difficult to get out of. Sentient beings who have committed the most grave evil deeds are born here. The suffering in this hell is experienced and perceived as: 1. no pause from unremitting sufferings; 2. no space as one's agony fills the entire place; 3. no intervals between various torturings; 4. no exemption to whoever has committed the evil deeds and 5. no break from continuous deaths and rebirths. Details are described in Ch. 3 of this sūtra. See *Avīci Hell*.

70 Filial means befitting a son or daughter, which is not thinking, speaking or acting negatively towards one's parents.

71 Dharma-doors-to-enlightenment, also known as "dharma entrances" (*dharma-paryāya*), refer to convenient means and effective ways of practice, such as those instructed in this sūtra, which will lead to further enlightenment. Some examples include burning incense, paying homage to the images of the Buddhas and Bodhisattvas, chanting their names, reading sūtras and so forth.

Chapter 2

72 "Unthinkable, indiscussable, immeasurable, unspeakable" are numeral concepts in ancient India referring to immense numbers far beyond

mundane numeral description. See *numerical units* in Glossary.

73 Kṣitigarbha Bodhisattva can divide (reproduce) Himself into an infinite number of identical entities which are exactly like Him, thus called "divided-identical" (*vigraha*) Kṣitigarbha Bodhisattvas.

74 *Anuttara-samyak-saṃbodhi* is Sanskrit for "unsurpassed, perfect and complete enlightenment". It refers to unexcelled, correct and complete awareness, the perfect wisdom of a Buddha. *Anuttara* means "highest" or "supreme"; *samyak* means "perfect", "true" and "proper"; *saṃbodhi* means "complete enlightenment". Such enlightened wisdom means one has the correct view and cognition of how each being feels and why the being thinks, speaks and acts the way he does in the past, present and future.

75 Sagehood here refers to either one of the four levels of sagehood in Hīnayāna or to a pratyeka-buddha. See *Three Vehicles* in Glossary.

76 "Root" in Buddhism can refer to two kinds of roots: the six sensory roots of the eyes, ears, nose, tongue, body and mind; and the "five virtuous roots" of faith, diligent advancement, focused thought (on dharma), samādhi and wisdom. See *roots* in Glossary.

77 Mundane blessings of humans can be categorized into three groups: 1. blessings of good health, appearance and longevity; 2. blessings of wealth (visible and invisible such as intelligence and capability); and 3. blessings directed toward having a good mission/destiny in one's life which brings results in being successful in terms of family, career and social standing.

78 A transformational entity (body) refers to one of the Buddhas' and Mahāsattvas' miraculous conveniences—the ability to appear in any form in order to save beings in the six realms of existence.

79 *Devarāja*: Sanskrit word for celestial king.

80 *Brahmarāja*, also known as *Lord Brahmā*, is the king of a Brahmā heaven in the celestial realm.

81 A wheel-turning king (*cakravartī*) is a bodhisattva of the 2nd stage. In the mundane world, he is an influential and virtuous leader who possesses the blessings of the Seven Royal Jewels and the merits to lead and educate his people away from the ten evils with the guidance of the Ten Virtuous Disciplines.

82   *Bhikṣu* and *bhikṣuṇī* are Sanskrit for "beggar" and refer to monks and nuns who have joined the saṃgha and renounced all mundane possessions, passions and mission to cultivate the mind of Bodhi.

83   *Upāsaka* or *upāsikā* are the Sanskrit words for male and female lay Buddhists who observe the Five Disciplines and are serious in their Buddhist practice. The Five Disciplines are: staying away from killing, stealing, sexual misconduct, deceptive speech (lying) and alcohol.

84   *Arhat* is Sanskrit for "one who is worthy". An Arhat is the highest-level practitioner of Hīnayāna (Small Vehicle) Buddhism and is free from reincarnation, the cycle of birth-death. See *Arhat* in Glossary.

85   The reasons for describing sentient beings of this time and on this earth as "obstinate, hard-to-tame, habitual evildoing, sinful and suffering" are found throughout this sūtra. It is the kind and merciful teaching from the Buddha to call attention to all of us. Here are several key quotes to shed light on the description:

Ch. 2: "For those who still have the habit to do evil... I have been diligently exerting various techniques to rescue those most obstinate, hard-to-tame, sinful, suffering beings."

Ch. 6: "...whenever their minds generate an idea or take any action, the idea and action are all karmic and sinful deeds."

Ch. 7: "...as soon as a thought or an idea is instigated, their driving force is nothing but sin. Even if they have gained some temporary relief [from their sinful sufferings] along with a few benefits, soon after they will lose their original wish of seeking liberation. When they encounter unfavorable conditions, [they fall back into their habitual-sinful-karmic ways and let] evil thoughts grow one after another."

"These sentient beings who are habitually inclined toward evil will always make some petty evil suddenly grow into an infinite and enormous one."

Ch. 8: "...soon after those beings are liberated from the retributions of their sins, they fall back into the evil realms again."

"The temperaments of sentient beings of Southern Jambudvīpa are characterized by extreme stubbornness and unwillingness to yield. They are very difficult to mediate and tame."

    The Sutra of Kṣitigarbha's Fundamental Vows

Ch. 13: "Even if they have generated some benevolent mind and thoughts, a moment later they will regress from that virtue again. When encountering unfavorable conditions, their minds [will lean towards evil, and that is the time the evil thoughts] will grow and expand continuously."

86   *Maitreya*, also known as *Ajita,* has been destined to be the next Buddha. *Maitreya* in Sanskrit means "benevolent" and "kind". This Mahāsattva is now expounding the dharma in the inner court of Tuṣita Heaven. See *Ajita* in Glossary.

87   *Nirvāṇa*: a state of infinity validated through cultivation of Buddhism in which there is no suffering, birth or death, only eternal bliss.

Chapter 3

88   For example, the world of *Amitābha Buddha* has no women and no beings of the lower three realms.

89   Southern *Jambudvīpa* (our world) will be without dharma once it passes through the Dharma-Declining Period and moves into the Dharma-Extinction Period.

90   In Amitābha Buddha's land, there are no women and sentient beings of the lower three paths. There are only men, śrāvakas, pratyeka-buddhas, bodhisattvas and the Buddha. In Fragrant-Amass Buddha's land, there are only men, bodhisattvas and the Buddha; there are no women, śrāvakas, pratyeka-buddhas or the three lower paths.

91   *Saṃgha* is Sanskrit for "assembly" or "multitude" and refers to a group of at least four monks or nuns who reside and practice together, observe the Ten Virtuous Disciplines and live by the "Six Points of Reverent Harmony" which refers to the practitioners' agreement and unity in action, speech and mind; observing the same disciplines; harmoniously upholding the Buddha's views; and equally sharing the dāna. Such unity will allow the saṃgha group to practice in harmony.

92   *Śramaṇa* is Sanskrit for an "ascetic and mendicant practitioner", referring to a Buddhist disciple admitted to monkhood (a monk) who has left home to cultivate renouncing mundane possessions, passions and mission and has vowed to observe the disciplines of the saṃgha for the purpose of realizing Bodhi.

93   Refers to those śramaṇas who pretend to be practitioners, but are not practitioners at heart, because they have not made the vow to seek true liberation according to the teachings of the Buddha.

94   Five Rebellious (Grave) Sins are: 1. patricide; 2. matricide; 3. killing an Arhat; 4. intentionally shedding the blood of a Buddha; and 5. causing disharmony in the saṃgha. Committing any of these sins leads to rebirth in Unremitting Hell.

Chapter 4

95   *Ajita* is Sanskrit for "invincible, unconquerable, irresistible". It is another name for Maitreya Bodhisattva Mahāsattva, the next Buddha. See *Maitreya* in Glossary.

96   Collective karma-fields: in any place or circumstance where two or more people start interacting with a shared goal or interest, collective invisible forces are formed and can influence participants' behaviors, such as in a family, on a battlefield, in a casino, on social media, on a football field, amidst a group, a society, or even a nation.

97   The five paths of celestial beings, humans, hungry ghosts, animals and hell beings. See *Six Paths* in Glossary and *Sahā World* map.

98   Also known as the ten characteristics or epithets of a Buddha. See *Ten Meritorious Designations of Tathāgata* in Glossary.

99   Here, the word "king" refers to a mundane leader who, in the Authentic-Dharma Period, is also a bodhisattva of the 1st stage because of his merits and wisdom; but in the Dharma-Declining and Dharma-Extinction Periods, most leaders no longer possess the needed merits. Therefore, they are not Bodhisattvas.

100 Cultivating the *Ten Virtuous Disciplines, Ten Disciplines* or *Ten Virtues* as defined by the Buddha results in beneficial blessings and leads to ultimate deliverance. All sentient beings are encouraged to refrain from committing the ten evil deeds in order to depart from suffering and gain happiness. Once we stay away from committing these harmful deeds, we are observing the ten virtuous disciplines and will thus gain the 71 benefits. Refer to *The Sūtra of the Path of Ten Virtuous Deeds*. See also *virtuous and evil deeds* and *Ten Evil Deeds* in Glossary.

   The Sutra of Kṣitigarbha's Fundamental Vows

101 *Bodhi* is Sanskrit for "awakening" or "enlightenment" and refers to the perfect wisdom, having understood, the way, and the truth. It denotes the wisdom of ending all delusions and afflictions and the realization of nirvāṇa. The bodhi of a Buddha is the ultimate, unsurpassed wisdom and is thus called *anuttara-samyak-saṃbodhi*—unsurpassed, perfect and complete enlightenment. One can achieve enlightenment through cultivating the Three Vehicles—*Hīnayāna* (Small), *Pratyeka-buddhayāna* or *Madhyamayāna* (Middle) and *Mahāyāna* (Great).

102 *Brahmacārī*: Sanskrit word for ascetic practitioner.

103 Sexual misconduct is one of the ten evil deeds defined by the Buddha as it will bring about harmful consequences and should be avoided. It refers to having sex out of wedlock and the retributions are having an unfaithful spouse and being foolish and ignorant.

104 Alienating speech refers to speech, gossip or any negative talk that will cause disharmony among two or more people or within and between groups, nations, etc.

105 *Mahāyāna* in Sanskrit is "Great Vehicle", one of the three cultivation methods in Buddhism. See *Mahāyāna* in Glossary.

106 *Sūtra* is a Sanskrit word meaning "thread"; in Buddhism it means "discourse" (as a type of Buddhist sacred text) and refers to collections of the Buddha's teachings.

107 The Four Celestial Kings each dwell on a side of Mount Sumeru; their kingdoms are situated on the 1st level of the Realm of Desire. They are guardians of humans and their kingdoms; they also guard the Buddha-dharma and shield sentient beings from the harm of evil gods and ghosts. They and their subordinates travel extensively to inspect and respond to virtuous or evil behaviors of all sentient beings. See *Four Celestial Kings* in Glossary and *Sahā World* map.

108 The two retributions of killing are a short lifespan and being annoyed and distressed. Refer to *The Sūtra of the Path of Ten Virtuous Deeds*.

109 Retributions for sexual misconduct—Magpies, sparrows, pigeons and mandarin ducks are mostly monogamous. When one spouse dies, the other one often lives alone. They are prey to other animals and live in constant hunger and fear.

110 Poaching the young refers to taking young animals away from their parents. In the case of animals, the purpose is either for personal

pleasure, for gourmet reasons or for profit, such as taking an unborn lamb from the womb for its soft skin. Humans also kidnap children as slaves, laborers, soldiers, etc.

111   "Having a hundred tongues" refers to beings such as cicadas and crickets, whose tongues vibrate a hundred times more rapidly than other beings, or skylarks and mockingbirds who mimic other beings' sounds.

Chapter 5

112   *Samantabhadra*, along with *Mañjuśrī*, are the two Mahāsattvas often depicted on either side of Śākyamuni Buddha. *Samantabhadra* in Sanskrit means "universal worthy". He is also most distinguished for leading those practicing the Path of Bodhisattva and considered the patron of the *Flower Ornament Sūtra*. See Glossary for details.

113   A Buddhist's conception of hell—It is a "classroom" for auditory and visual education, not a place for punishment; it is not designed by a higher deity, but manifested by the sinful deeds of each sentient being; and it's not permanent. It is a place where Kṣitigarbha Bodhisattva frequents to offer His salvation. The purpose of discussing the various hells is to warn sentient beings not to commit evil deeds so that they can avoid falling into those horrendous hells and also to urge them to see the necessity of being close to Kṣitigarbha Bodhisattva for His imminent rescue and of observing the ten virtuous disciplines. See *Hells & Karmic Seas* map.

114   In Howling Hell, sinful beings are sounding out their suffering of great pain and distress.

115   "Take homage in the Buddha". In Sanskrit, *Buddha* means the "Enlightened One". When we pay homage to a Buddha, it means that we honor, seek help and take refuge in wisdom. It also means that through the process of re-examining the experiences of our lives (i.e. our actions, speech and thoughts) as well as reflecting those of others back to ourselves according to the Buddha-dharma, we comprehend the causes of our suffering and happiness, our virtues and evils, and life's truths and falsities. The ultimate goal is to become a Buddha, with complete enlightened-wisdom and strength.

   The Sutra of Kṣitigarbha's Fundamental Vows

Chapter 6

116 Non-humans generally refer to low-level ghosts and gods of the Eight Legions usually led by asuras. Their duties are to protect the Buddha-dharma and encourage Buddhist practitioners. See *Eight Legions* in Glossary.

117 The name *Samantavipula* means "universal extensive". Later in this chapter, the Buddha entrusts this Bodhisattva with the important task of circulating and advocating this sūtra. In addition to this noble task, Samantavipula Bodhisattva asks questions on behalf of all sentient beings.

118 Due to the lack of clarity in the Chinese scripture and the inability on our part to verify the author's meaning in the original recording, our best research indicates the phrase "for the time span of having a meal" can have two meanings: 1. paying tribute to Kṣitigarbha Bodhisattva for a short while can have abundant benefits; or 2. after paying tribute as instructed, her misery, in her perception, will pass as quickly as the time it takes to have a meal. Please keep in mind the prerequisites of this woman's conditions: she strongly detests her ugliness and has been tormented by prolonged illness. These two factors will give her the momentum and desperation to pray, and this determines the effectiveness of the rescue.

119 Excellent features refer to having fine skin and a well-formed body in good health. From head to toe, her appearance will be graceful.

120 "Be spared from frequently hearing about any events of horror" does not mean that the person is ignorant or turning a deaf ear to the disasters that occur every day in the world. Rather, the person does not think of these events as "harmful" or "bad" which would fan up indulgent and negative emotions. Instead, the person takes those events as reminders, being inspired to guide the mind for repentance and empathy so as to expand the mind and blessings. By doing so, it is called turning a bad thing into a beneficial one, or "turning a dharma wheel" in Buddhist terms.

121 *Bhadra Kalpa* (Kalpa of Sages or Auspicious Kalpa) is the name for the present kalpa. In each kalpa, there are 1,000 Buddhas who make their presence known. Śākyamuni is the 4th Buddha of this kalpa, and Maitreya Bodhisattva Mahāsattva (Ajita) will be the next Buddha.

122 Hungry ghost is one of the three lower realms (paths). Being born in this realm is the ill consequence for stinginess and greed. Within this realm, there are several categories (sub-realms) according to the severities of the sins and each has different kinds of suffering. Hungry ghosts are tormented by constant, insatiable hunger and thirst, wandering hopelessly in search of sensual fulfillment.

123 *Yamarāja* is the king of Suyāma Heaven as well as the controller of hells and their ghosts—thus, he has double identities and double responsibilities. *Yamarāja* informs and announces where newly deceased beings will reincarnate after reviewing the deeds these beings committed in their most recent lifetime. *Yama* in Sanskrit means "double" (as in identical) or "twin" and also refers to equal and fairness as he treats all sentient beings equally and fairly, according to the severity of their sins, regardless of their previous identities or where they came from. *Rāja* means "king". There is more discussion in Ch. 8 about Yamarāja.

124 Reading the sūtra aloud has another purpose and benefit other than letting the dying one hear the sūtra teachings. It also enables the relatives to shoulder the responsibility required to be representatives of the Buddha. Their responsibility is to recite the sūtra to the dying one and to other sentient beings, mostly low-level ghosts and gods in the invisible world, so they can take homage in the Three Jewels. These ghosts and gods in the invisible world are likely the foes of the dying one. Thus, if they take homage in the Three Jewels, they would refrain from causing harm or hardship while the dying one embarks upon the new journey towards the next rebirth.

125 In ancient times, copying sūtras by hand was one of the ways to re-produce sūtra texts for circulation before modern printing technology was invented. Nowadays, hand-copying sūtras is sometimes observed as a way to learn the sūtra with respect and thus gain greater benefit.

126 *Kṣatriya* was the second highest caste in ancient India, comprised of kings and royal family members as well as civil and military officers. Brahmans were the most prestigious citizens, dominating religious matters and knowledge. See *brahman* in Glossary.

127 A baby born with evil karma means that the baby will encounter more illnesses and misfortunes, perhaps even a short lifespan, and also be difficult to care for.

     The Sutra of Kṣitigarbha's Fundamental Vows

128 Fasting refers to the discipline of eating rather than simply abstaining from food. On fasting days, practitioners shall observe taking one meal a day before noontime, preferably vegetarian without pungent vegetables and alcohol. This observation is also to help lay Buddhists learn and emulate the practice of the saṃgha in the temple. Fasting days are related to the full moon, half-moon and new moon. They are the 1st, 8th, 14th, 15th, 18th, 23rd, 24th, 28th, 29th and the 30th days of each month of the lunar calendar according to this sūtra.

129 Since little is known about India's ancient calendar, we can only go by the lunar calendar.

130 The Four (Grave) Prohibitions refer to staying away from the deeds of killing, stealing, sexual misconduct and deception, including untruthful speech or telling lies. The Buddha revealed to us about these four grave, evil deeds so that we could avoid the grave, evil consequences. Since ancient times, mankind has undisputedly shared the common view that these four deeds are to be prohibited or avoided in order to regulate our mind, behavior and social order.

131 *Gāthā* is a Sanskrit word meaning "song", "verse" or "stanza". It is an enriched form of dharma teaching that can be chanted or sung to practice mindfulness. This was a popular practice in ancient India.

Chapter 7

132 The temporary relief and benefits come from sentient beings' efforts in seeking immediate help from Kṣitigarbha Bodhisattva for His rescue and protection, such as making a "911" emergency call.

133 The range of dependents includes parents, spouses, siblings, children, colleagues, servants, friends and close acquaintances.

134 Knowledge and frequent chanting of the names of the Buddha and Kṣitigarbha Bodhisattva will have a decisive effect at the time of death, so that the dying ones can follow the guidance of the Three Jewels without being misled into the evil paths by evil ghosts and spirits. Also, with consistent chanting, they will be spared of shock, anxiety and confusion.

135 At the time of death, most sentient beings are in a state of confusion and shock, often without a clear destination or assistance. To let go

of their bodies and their loved ones can be very difficult. Sūtra reading and chanting can help them to focus upon and pursue help from the most virtuous entities—the Buddha and Kṣitigarbha Bodhisattva—so that the journey of rebirth can be well-guided and uplifted.

136 "Seed of Bodhi" refers to the seed of enlightenment from the initial connection with the Three Jewels through hearing Kṣitigarbha's name, seeing His image and knowing His merits.

137 The "invisible, in-between state" refers to the intermediate existence (*antarā-bhava*) between death and the following rebirth, lasting up to 49 days. In this state, there is no physical or visible body, but the mind continues to function seeking a new identity and new place to be reincarnated. This invisible, in-between state is similar to our dream state—when our physical body is not actively looking, listening, smelling, tasting, touching or moving, yet the dream is vividly "real". The entity in the invisible, in-between state (or the dream state) has supernatural powers across time and space.

138 A Mahāsattva, Great Eloquence's name in Sanskrit is *Mahāprati-bhāna*, referring to one with the merit of having great, convenient and enlightening speech. *Mahā* means "great"; *pratibhāna* means "eloquence", "readiness of wit" and "presence of mind".

139 The *Dharma of No-Birth* is the merit and capacity of a bodhisattva who has passed the 6th stage among a total of ten stages (on the Path of Bodhisattva). At the 7th, 8th and 9th stages, a bodhisattva has gained insight and penetrated deeply into the true nature of existence with non-dualistic wisdom and validated that all existences have no beginning and no end (or are non-arisen and non-destroyed). Hence, his endurance capacity of mind enters directly into the elimination of controversy and the absence of obstacles, thus continuing to realize the truthful realm of all phenomena and dwelling in it with no-regression.

Chapter 8

140 Ghost kings are closely related with the well-being of humans and other sentient beings, overseeing matters and events (such as calamities, dangers, wealth, diseases, destinies, birthing, food and

　　　　The Sutra of Kṣitigarbha's Fundamental Vows

animals) along with their subordinates. They either bless or don't bless, depending on the being's virtuous or evil deeds; they do not "punish".

141 *Ghost King of Wasted-Blessings* checks on people to see if sentient beings are indulging and wasting their blessings, or if they are ungratefully claiming credit for themselves instead of giving gratitude to their benefactors such as their parents and those in the invisible realm. Such deeds will offend the Ghost King of Wasted-Blessings, which will deplete their blessings quickly.

142 *Ghost King of Disasters* takes charge of all accidents and disasters. Usually, several ghost kings and their subordinates are working together to induce a disaster according to the evil deeds of those involved. They weigh the virtuous or evil deeds of these people which determine the severity and the outcomes of the disaster. For instance, an airline accident involves Ghost King of Disasters, Calamity-Spreading Ghost King, Ghost King of Destiny, Ghost King of Danger and/or Ghost King of Wasted-Blessings. This explains why many people can die in an accident, while some survive without a scratch.

143 *Ghost King of Food* takes charge of whether the sentient beings have ample and delicious food or lack of it.

144 *Ghost King of Beasts* takes charge of the well-being of non-domestic, four-legged animals including mice.

145 *Ghost King of Birthing* takes charge of the well-being of pregnant mothers, fetuses and their delivery including miscarriages, premature births, difficult births and birth-related illnesses.

146 *Ghost King of Destiny* takes charge of life, from birth to death, and the well-being of all sentient beings. He is also a Mahāsattva.

147 *Ghost King of Disease* takes charge of major and minor illnesses, determining whether they are fatal and painful or not.

148 *Ghost King of Danger* takes charge of how many dangers and its severities a being will encounter during a lifetime.

149 *Three-Eyed Ghost King, Four-Eyed Ghost King* and *Five-Eyed Ghost King* have to do with our eyesight, which is one of the most important "roots" (organs) among our six senses, and most prone to committing evil deeds. The additional eyes of these ghost kings are for the purpose of detecting our pretenses and wrongdoings.

150 The names of *Qi-li-shi Ghost King* and the following five ghost kings (*Great Qi-li-shi Ghost King, Qi-li-cha Ghost King, Great Qi-li-cha Ghost King, Ana-zha Ghost King* and *Great Ana-zha Ghost King*) are phonetic spellings from Chinese characters; their Sanskrit spellings and exact responsibilities are not clear to us at the present time.

151 There are two reasons that *Yamarāja* turns and looks at Kṣitigarbha Bodhisattva. The first reason is to salute Kṣitigarbha with his glance, and the second reason is to exchange a knowing look, a look of recognition, as Yamarāja is a transformational entity of Kṣitigarbha Bodhisattva—they are actually one entity. He is also known as *Deva Yamarāja*.

152 "Either benefit humans or harm them". Describes the ghost kings' jurisdictions as perceived by humans. Ghost kings interact with sentient beings according to the Law of Cause and Consequence— "performing virtuous deeds will harvest blessings; committing evil deeds will suffer misfortunes". They either bless or don't bless, depending on the being's virtuous or evil deeds. Great ghost kings are Bodhisattvas, even Mahāsattvas, who wear two hats with twofold tasks. Even if the ghost kings' appearances seem frightful or terrifying, they mean well and their hearts are kind and merciful—regardless of how they look, their only wish is for sentient beings to depart from evil deeds to gain benefits. However, because we are obstinate, hard-to-tame, habitual evildoing and sinful beings with minds unyielding and difficult to turn, we always neglect the ghost kings' "ferocious looks", which are their merciful warnings. Therefore, one will inevitably harvest and suffer the ill consequences of ones' evil deeds and perceive it as punishment, when it is actually the result of cause-consequence.

153 Human beings are interconnected with ghosts and gods, especially lower-level evil ghosts and gods, according to each human's karmic deeds. The duties of ghosts and gods are to give "punishment" or blessings (i.e. not to confuse, disturb or ridicule) to humans according to each person's evil or virtuous deeds which in turn increases the ghosts and gods' strength towards virtue or evil. Therefore, ghosts and gods appreciate and are pleased to see humans perform virtuous deeds. Also, humans have more merits than lower-level evil ghosts and gods and usually don't encounter or mingle with them as they are meant to be kept in two separate realms. However, when one's mind is dark, troubled, ill or with heavy karma, one would attract them and induce unnecessary, evil entanglement.

                          The Sutra of Kṣitigarbha's Fundamental Vows

154 *Lord Brahmā* and *Lord Śakra* are protectors of humans, especially Buddhist practitioners. Lord Brahmā is the king of a Brahmā heaven. Lord Śakra is the king of Trāyastriṃśa Heaven and a Bodhisattva of the 3rd stage; he is often challenged by asuras.

155 *Lord of Land* is one of the subordinates of *God of Solid-Firm-Earth* (see Ch. 11) overseeing the well-being of sentient beings within a particular area or district.

156 "To benefit and give me the needed strength". Ghost kings either bless or don't bless; they do not "punish". Moreover, they discourage humans from worshipping them and their subordinates. Instead, ghost kings urge sentient beings to praise and pay homage to the Three Jewels, the Buddha and Kṣitigarbha Bodhisattva to not only increase their virtuous strength but also for us humans to gain more capital to realize emancipation, as the ghost kings would do the same for themselves too.

157 Here *Ghost King of Destiny* gives a strong warning not to follow "deceased relatives" at the time of death. Sentient beings have the tendency to entangle with relatives and old acquaintances, which gives evil ghosts the opportunity to trick dying ones onto evil paths. Our deceased relatives, after forty-nine days of their deaths, start their journeys of reincarnation and no longer remember their past.

Chapter 9

158 The Buddhas represent absolute beauty, absolute virtue and absolute truth. Chanting their names will turn on the mechanism in our minds to pursue beauty, virtue and truth, and move away from ugliness, evil and illusion. In order to elevate ourselves so as to achieve the desired effects, we also need to contemplate the merits of those Buddhas when chanting their names.

159 Boundless-Body (*Anantakāya*) refers to a Buddha whose body is infinite without boundaries. A body without boundaries is hard to imagine, let alone to sculpt or paint. Contemplating *Anantakāya*'s image gives us the opportunity to break through our sensory limitations which are extremely inferior. Our mind can go beyond these limitations if we contemplate this Buddha's name, which will lead us into the realm of the infinite, invisible world.

160 Precious-Nature (*Ratna-maya*) refers to a Buddha with the most distinct merit of treasuring the essence or nature of a Buddha. The precious nature of a Buddha is true permanence, true bliss, true self and true purity. Because of these characteristics, we can rely on this Buddha, take refuge in Him and pay homage to Him in order to bring out the same characteristics and qualities in us.

161 "Dharma king" refers to a Buddha who, with his unsurpassed wisdom, has realized all dharma. Thus, he is the mentor, role model, teacher and rescuer of all sentient beings.

162 Superb Red-Lotus (*Padmottara*) refers to a Buddha who realized complete Buddhahood like a red lotus growing out of a muddy swamp. See *Superb-Red-Lotus Tathāgata* in Glossary.

163 *Heaven of Six Desires* covers six different levels of heavens where the sensory pleasures of the eyes, ears, nose, tongue and body (touch) are extraordinarily superb. In other words, the sights, sounds, smell, taste and bodily sensations are truly beyond human imagination.

164 Roaring-Lion (*Siṃhanāda*) refers to a Buddha who, like a roaring lion with his powerful and majestic voice, awakens sentient beings whose minds are in a delusional state.

165 *Krakucchanda* (Firmly-Stop-Evil-and-Act-Virtuously) refers to the 4th of the "Seven Buddhas of Antiquity" as well as the 1st Buddha of the present Bhadra Kalpa—the Kalpa of Sages. This Buddha has the merit to lead sentient beings to know what is virtuous and what is evil; what deeds are to be done and what deeds need to be avoided. In other words, He is pure in upholding the ten virtuous disciplines.

166 Lord Mahā-brahma is a devarāja in the celestial path who rules over the Brahmā worlds (the first dhyāna heavens) and is a Bodhisattva of the 8th or 9th stage. Along with Lord Śakra, he protects Buddhist practitioners and humans. See *Sahā World* map.

167 *Vipaśyin* (Correct-Contemplation) refers to a Buddha who has the merits of correct contemplation and observation without any barrier or interference. Chanting His name frequently will prevent us from falling into the three evil paths. *Vipaśyin* is also the 1st Buddha of the "Seven Buddhas of Antiquity".

168 Abundant-Jewels (*Prabhūta-ratna*) means that this Buddha's most distinct merit is to enable all sentient beings to have the abundant and superb treasures of the Buddha-dharma.

169 Precious-Appearance (*Ratna-ketu*) means that this Buddha is most distinct for His superb appearance and overall image as a Buddha. In other words, His deeds of thinking, speech and action are excellent and stainless.

170 Banner-of-a-Monk's-Robe (*Kāṣāya-dhvaja*) refers to a Buddha who upholds the banner of "being a monk in a monk's robe" signifying deliverance in the mundane world. It is a metaphor for being victorious in taming demons and foes that are in one's mind. Being a monk signifies the excellent merits of leaving the mundane way of living and becoming part of the saṃgha to pursue the ultimate enlightenment as a Buddha.

171 Great Penetration Mountain King (*Mahābhijña-parvata-rāja*) refers to a Buddha who has the merits of penetrating and breaking down all barriers, making obstructions disappear. Without the barriers of the ten evil deeds, one can achieve true equality and supreme wisdom.

172 Pure-Moon Buddha (*Śuddha-candra*). In Sanskrit, *śuddha* means "pure", "stainless" and "clean"; *candra* means "moon" and "bright". Buddhist sūtras frequently use the moon to represent a state of purity, tranquility and a feeling of renewal, away from a sense of burning agitation or trouble.

Chapter 10

173 From this chapter onwards, Kṣitigarbha and other major participants in this great assembly tell the mundane leaders and virtuous men and women how to perform dāna so they can receive blissful merits that will enable them to advance to become bodhisattvas. This is in major contrast with the previous chapters where we were guided to examine our sinful, evil deeds that have caused, or will cause, great suffering. The purpose of those chapters was to instigate in us the much-needed alarm or fear so we would vow to refrain from doing evil deeds and make close connections with the Three Jewels and Kṣitigarbha in order to gain their guidance, protection and blessing.

174 These kings and mundane leaders are those who have cultivated virtuous deeds in their past lifetimes and are thus currently enjoying great blessings as leaders.

175 Seven Royal Jewels (*saptaratna*) symbolize the virtues and blessings of a wheel-turning king whose seven attributes appear automatically and come in the form of a golden wheel (*cakraratna*), his state elephant, charger horse, divine jewel (an octagonal gem so luminous it can light his army's path by night), his queen, treasury ministers (lay Buddhists) and defense ministers (advisors and generals).

176 Here the pleasures refer to the sensory pleasures of the Five Desires— having beautiful scenes to satisfy the eyes, pleasant sounds to satisfy the ears, superb smells to please the nose, exquisite tastes to satisfy the tongue and pleasing sensations to satisfy the body.

177 Attributing the merits is a conceptual process of sharing the blessings and benefits with other beings. It is one of the most important practices in Mahāyāna Buddhism. The purpose of it is to expand our mind by including others in our consideration and breaking the barriers that separate "I" from all other people, beings and the Buddhas. Buddhism believes that all beings in the ten dharma realms share the same mind, thus there should not be any self-centered segregation among all beings. It is also the best way to accumulate "capital" to become enlightened.

178 Dharma realms refer to the ten realms or paths of sentient beings. See *dharma realms* in Glossary.

179 The Pure Abodes (*Śuddhāvāsa*) are the five highest heavens in the Realm of Form: Heaven of No Trouble, Heaven of No Heat, Heaven of Virtuous Views, Heaven of Virtuous Manifestations and Ultimate Form Heaven. See *Sahā World* map.

180 "Planting virtuous roots" is a term frequently used in Buddhism. It means once a seed is planted, roots and sprouts grow, which develop into a plant or a tree, bearing flowers and fruits that are beneficial and enjoyable. Doing virtuous deeds according to the Buddha's teachings sets virtuous roots which will bring about benefits in the future.

181 "Dāna to Mahāyāna sūtras" is aligning our mind with the sūtra which is considered *dāna of dharma*, the highest level of the three kinds of dāna. "Dāna to Mahāyāna sūtras" means to study, practice and validate the teachings and to help others to do the same. In general, dāna to the Three Jewels is the most beneficial offering one can do in the mundane world. See *dāna* in Glossary.

     The Sutra of Ksitigarbha's Fundamental Vows

182 *Dānapati* is Sanskrit for a generous donor who strongly supports
Buddhist matters.

Chapter 11

183 God of Solid-Firm-Earth (*Dṛḍha-pṛthivī-devatā*). *Dṛḍha* means "firm,
strong, unswerving, durable, reliable"; *pṛthivī* means "earth"; *devatā*
means "god". It refers to the god of the great earth that nurtures
and provides all the wealth that we need, such as crops, minerals and
water; the earth also bears and supports all the establishments above
and under the ground. This powerful god is one of the best representatives as well as a divided-identical body of Kṣitigarbha Bodhisattva Mahāsattva.

184 *Avalokiteśvara* in Sanskrit means "Lord Who Gazes Down (at the
World)" or "He Who Hears the Sounds (Outcries) of the World".
This Mahāsattva is from Amitābha Buddha's Pure Land, most
distinguished for His great mercy. He also has a deep, intimate
connection with sentient beings in Jambudvīpa and listens and
answers to their sufferings prevalently. *Avalokiteśvara* is greatly
venerated universally and also known as Bodhisattva of Compassion,
Goddess of Mercy, Guanyin (China), Kannon (Japan), Chenrezig
(Tibet) and Lokesvara (Thailand and Cambodia). See Ch. 12.

185 "Land is fertile" means that plants will grow well with good harvest,
even without cultivation, and likely some minerals or treasures will
come forth from the land.

186 A safe household is free from any natural disasters, such as storms and
earthquakes. Furthermore, there won't be any accidents and harm,
such as illness or disturbances, dispatched from evil ghosts and gods.

187 Those who practice the teachings of Kṣitigarbha Bodhisattva will
face disasters and unpleasant events with a very different mentality.
They will not see these events as "unexpected harm", but rather as a
reminder of the Eight Sufferings in this mundane world, so to generate
a vow to depart from the sufferings through cultivating the Path of
Bodhisattva.

188   The term "fine rays" is difficult to visualize. The closest description is to contemplate when sunrays pass through a small crevice into a dark room, and there are many highly condensed, small light particles dancing and radiating afar. The energy of these rays is most enchanting and impressive. The rays that Bhagavat radiated were under broad daylight, coupled with profound dharma.

189   The merit of "saving others" means to rescue the infinite and boundless number of sentient beings in the six realms. "Advancing himself" means that while saving others by understanding their minds and finding convenient ways to help change their mentalities, he also understands that others' minds are part of his own mental process and realization, and in this way, he advances.

190   Only when a bodhisattva reaches the 8th stage on the Path of Bodhisattva will he not regress; when he reaches the 10th stage, he will soon become a Buddha. In other words, the Path of Bodhisattva is the path of becoming a Buddha. Here, Śākyamuni Buddha announces that Kṣitigarbha Bodhisattva has already validated the wisdom of *Sarvajña* (the wisdom of a Buddha), yet He chooses to remain a Bodhisattva Mahāsattva so as to benefit sentient beings.

191   The five signs of decay for celestial beings shortly before death are: 1. clothing turned filthy; 2. flowers on crown of head wither; 3. sweating in armpits; 4. foul bodily odor; and 5. uneasiness with anxiety. Celestial beings do not necessarily go through aging and ailing, but they do go through the process of birth and dying. Unlike the vivid and slow aging and dying process in humans, with celestial beings, death can occur suddenly without forewarning, and the impact is so strong that it can create resentment or even hatred, which would be the cause of their reincarnating in evil realms.

192   For those who have lost a parent or sibling, there are three different levels of beneficial results depending on their wish and the Buddhist service that they perform.

193   The (burning) Three Realms are the three levels of realms in the Sahā World. Sentient beings are born in one of these realms as consequences of their deeds:

1. *Realm of Desire* which includes the six heavens of desire, the human path, asura path and the lower three evil paths;

2. *Realm of Form*, a world of superb virtuous blessings without the confusion of desires; and

3. *Realm of Formlessness*, a pure transcendent world without the presence of any form. See *Sahā World* map.

Although the upper realms are more blissful than the human realm, the bliss is not permanent, and the suffering of reincarnation will arrive like a house on fire.

The term "Burning Three Realms" originates in the *Lotus Sūtra*, Ch. 3. In this sūtra, the Buddha tells a metaphor about an elderly man trying to persuade his children to leave a run-down house that was on fire. But his children were so involved in their play that they were oblivious to the danger. Thus, the elder had to lure them out by telling them there were carriages of goat, deer and ox waiting for them outside, and he succeeded. What was actually waiting outside was a very splendid carriage pulled by a white ox. Symbolically, the Buddha is the elderly man, the goat, deer and ox are the Three Vehicles, the white ox is the supreme great Mahāyāna, we sentient beings are his children, and the burning house is the world we are in.

194 Five pungent vegetables refer to vegetables that can cause bad breath or gas and disturb the peacefulness of the mind. Also, they are considered stimulants and trigger desires. If eaten raw, these herbs could incite anger or disputes; if eaten cooked, it could lead to sexual desire and passion. Therefore, practitioners always abstain from and lay Buddhists, during fasting days, avoid eating these vegetables. They include: garlic, onion, scallion, chives and leek (any onion family) as well as asafoetida (stinking gum) and rape (mustard family).

Chapter 13

195 Space Treasury (*Ākāśagarbha*) Bodhisattva is a Mahāsattva and a close partner of Kṣitigarbha (Earth Treasury) Bodhisattva as the livelihood of all sentient beings is intimately related with earth and space.

196 The saintly stages refer to the stages of cultivation on the Path of Bodhisattva. Here it means when practicing Buddhism, one will swiftly pass through the *Hīnayāna* four stages (Small Vehicle), *Pratyeka-buddhayāna* stage (Middle Vehicle) to the *Mahāyāna* stage from pre-Bodhisattva (prior to the 1st stage) up through the ten stages on the Path of Bodhisattva (Great Vehicle) to become a Buddha.

Study Guide

The Sūtra of Kṣitigarbha's Fundamental Vows
Ten Key Points

From a teaching by
Master Sheng Chang Hwang

In *The Sūtra of Kṣitigarbha's Fundamental Vows*, all the dharma taught by the Buddha and various Bodhisattvas are exquisitely profound and hard to believe, not to mention difficult to comprehend. [After years of Buddhist practice, my fellow practitioners and I have come to the realization that] these minds of ours are petty, dull and of little faith, and we are too limited to absorb and hold much grand dharma. Nevertheless, please allow me to share the points of emphasis that my petty mind finds relevant.

1. This Sūtra is addressed to You and Me.

The assembly in Trāyastriṃśa Heaven is originally gathered for the sake of Lady Māyā, mother of Prince Siddhārtha. When Kṣitigarbha Bodhisattva Mahāsattva appears, the nature of that assembly is changed to address all sentient beings in this Dharma-Declining Period (this era) in southern Jambudvīpa (this earth) because the teachings are exactly what we need to hear. Therefore, this assembly is set to include you and me, and this Sūtra is most important for all of us.

During the assembly, the Buddha, Kṣitigarbha Bodhisattva Mahāsattva, other Bodhisattvas and many ghost kings describe us sentient beings of this time and this earth as: "obstinate, hard-to-tame, habitual evildoing, sinful, suffering beings" because they have observed that we possess the following characteristics:

(1) All our actions and thoughts are flawed, and we
    are prone to evil deeds and sin.

(2) Occasionally a virtuous thought is generated, but it
    fades away very fast; even when benefits are gained,
    the original kindness recesses rapidly. If unfortunate
    conditions arise, the evil deeds will appear one
    after another.

(3) Although Kṣitigarbha Bodhisattva Mahāsattva
    comes to our rescue again and again, we continue
    to fall into desperate situations repeatedly.

For the above three reasons, we *all* possess the characteristics of "obstinate, hard-to-tame, habitual evildoing, sinful, suffering beings." Therefore, we become the primary audience to be enlightened by this Sūtra, and we are the prime targets for Kṣitigarbha Bodhisattva Mahāsattva's salvation and illumination.

2. Knowing the Dharma of "What is Suffering and What is Happiness" is our initial connection with the Three Jewels.

This Sūtra has made it very clear from the very beginning that sentient beings of this era and earth are obstinate and hard-to-tame, because we fail to learn the dharma of what is suffering and what is happiness. Thus, we fail to make close connections with the Three Jewels.

In order to make close connections with the Three Jewels, the sequence of studies that will lead to a fruitful result is:

(1) Start from knowing and truly agreeing with the
    dharma on "suffering and happiness" according to

    The Sutra of Ksitigarbha's Fundamental Vows

the Buddha's viewpoint. Once we do that, we have
made a primary connection with the Three Jewels.

(2) Advance further from knowing the dharma of
"suffering and happiness" to learning the dharma
of "virtue and evil" in order to have a closer
connection with the Three Jewels.

(3) If we can further advance from knowing the dharma
of "virtue and evil" to knowing the dharma of
"true-false and right-wicked", then we will have a
tighter connection with the Three Jewels.

Unfortunately, as "obstinate, hard-to-tame, habitual evildoing, sinful, suffering beings", we are indifferent to the dharma of "what is happiness and what is suffering" as the Buddha teaches it. We are also unable to differentiate what is "true suffering" and what is "true happiness". Thus, we are unable to differentiate what is truly virtuous and what is truly evil, much less understand the dharma of "true-false and right-wicked". And consequently, we are unable to take homage in the Three Jewels, and we live forever in a state of delusion, upside-downness, murkiness, ignorance and stupidity such that our wisdom is blocked from revealing itself. This is a very important reminder provided by *The Sūtra of Kṣitigarbha's Fundamental Vows*.

3. Knowing the Dharma of "Suffering and Happiness" is learning the Dharma of the Four Noble Truths.

How can we learn the dharma of "suffering and happiness"?

We need to reflect on: why we suffered in the past, why we are suffering now, what will be our suffering in the future and why all sentient beings suffer. After we have a truthful understanding of "suffering", then we can match our own suffering with those of all sentient beings using the Eight Sufferings as a guideline—the suffering of birth and living, aging, ailing, dying, parting with the loved, meeting with the hated, unable to have wishes fulfilled and being in constant agitation. Only then will we be connected with the *Truth of Suffering*, the **First Noble Truth**.

If we further ask the questions: "How have all these sentient beings and I magnetized these sufferings? What have we done to bring about and manifest these sufferings? How do we suffer these sufferings? How do we react to these sufferings?" To find out the causes of these sufferings, we need to learn about the *Ten Evils* and the *Dharma of Twelve Links of Dependent Origination—Leading to Existence*. This is the beginning of differentiating the dharma of "virtue and evil". Once we have a correct re-cognition about suffering, we enter the *Truth of Magnetization*, the **Second Noble Truth**.

When we comprehend the truth of suffering and stop the magnetization, then all the causes of suffering as well as the bitter fruit of suffering will cease forever. This is the *Truth of Cessation*, the **Third Noble Truth**.

Then we can step up with another question: Is there any way all sentient beings and I can depart from all the suffering? And can we forever stop attracting such suffering? Does such a wonderful possibility truly exist? What kinds of "ways" or "paths" will bring us to that superb state?

Since we know there is the Path of Ten Virtuous Deeds and the ways of cultivation via the Three Vehicles, how can we correctly walk onto these paths?

    The Sutra of Ksitigarbha's Fundamental Vows

If we can make a vow to cultivate these ways, then we are engaging in the ***Truth of the Path***, the **Fourth Noble Truth**, which is the way to depart from suffering and gain happiness.

The Sūtra of Kṣitigarbha's Fundamental Vows can conveniently guide us from knowing the dharma of "suffering and happiness" to knowing the dharma of the Four Noble Truths. Furthermore, with this understanding, we can swiftly take homage in Kṣitigarbha Bodhisattva Mahāsattva and the Three Jewels.

4. Kṣitigarbha Bodhisattva Mahāsattva is the Prime Representative of the Dharma of the Strength of Vows.

Because we are obstinate, hard-to-tame, habitual evildoing, sinful, suffering beings, we are quite accustomed to living with this mentality and in the endless cycle of "sin-evil-suffering". Thus, we continue to manufacture evil deeds of thinking, speaking and acting without the ability nor willingness to correctly understand the dharma of suffering and happiness. As a result, we will never get to know the dharma of the Four Noble Truths. Consequently, we are forever under the dominance of the *force of karma*.

The teachings in this Sūtra reveal four past lives of Kṣiti garbha Bodhisattva that enable us to re-claim that even Kṣitigarbha Bodhisattva Mahāsattva had to rely on the *strength of vows* as the only way and means to overcome the force of karma. As long as we are willing, our future can be guided by the strength of vows and be free from the dominating force of karma; in addition, we can forever leave the karmic track to gain true freedom and true deliverance.

The Sūtra of Kṣitigarbha's Fundamental Vows tells us that Kṣitigarbha Bodhisattva Mahāsattva is the prime representative of the vows of all Bodhisattvas and Buddhas in the ten directions of this infinite universe throughout the past, present and future. Kṣitigarbha Bodhisattva Mahāsattva also represents the *"fundamental wishes"* of all sentient beings in the six realms which are to "avoid ill-fortune and gain good fortune; depart from suffering and gain happiness" as well as to pursue "permanence, happiness, true identity and purity". Therefore, all sentient beings need to take homage in the grand vows of Kṣitigarbha Bodhisattva Mahāsattva.

5. Knowing the Invisible World.

This Sūtra informs us that the dominant forces from the invisible world are far greater than the forces of the visible world, and the destiny of all sentient beings in the visible world is totally controlled by this invisible world.

What is this "invisible world"?

Any existence that cannot be recognized by our six senses—the eyes, ears, nose, tongue, body and mind as well as those existences that we fail to see, hear, smell, taste, touch and think—is present in the invisible world.

Thus, for sentient beings like us with petty minds, dull sensory roots and little faith, the invisible world includes all the Buddhas, bodhisattvas, pratyeka-buddhas, arhats, ghosts, gods, demons and the majority of sentient beings in the lower three realms. It also includes places that we haven't traveled to, events that we haven't experienced and humans whom we don't know, including ourselves.

          The Sutra of Ksitigarbha's Fundamental Vows

Why do we say that all humans, including ourselves, are in the invisible world?

Just think about this "mind" of ours: it has no appearance, no shape, no smell, no taste and is very elusive. Doesn't that belong to the world of the invisible? How about the three poisonous fires of the mind"? And how about our past and future lives? Don't they belong to the invisible world? Are we aware of the presence of all sentient beings? What has happened to the past and the future of our loved ones? Do we know their "minds"? Don't these all exist in the world of the invisible?

The world of the invisible is extremely vast and profound. It possesses immense power. It is the source of all energies, and it controls the destinies of all sentient beings in the visible world; only we are ignorant, unaware and insensitive to such an operation!

The Sūtra of Kṣitigarbha's Fundamental Vows helps us to comprehend, experience and acknowledge that the invisible world is very powerful, while the visible world that we normally consider powerful is actually quite impotent.

6. The "Ten Virtues and Ten Evils" is the link from the Visible World to the Invisible World.

All sentient beings who commit the Ten Evil Deeds must endure the Eight Sufferings. If they stay away from the Ten Evil Deeds, they are practicing the Ten Virtuous Deeds and can thus depart from suffering and gain happiness.

However, the dharma of virtue and evil exists mostly in the invisible world, especially the deeds of thought (arrogance with erroneous views, greed and stinginess, hatred and jealousy). Although the deeds of speech (deceptive speech, alienating speech, ill-intended speech and frivolous speech) and the deeds of action (killing, stealing and sexual misconduct) are more visible, as soon as we try to cover them up, they will fade into the invisible world.

When the ten evil deeds or the ten virtuous deeds gain enough momentum, they will come into the visible world from the invisible. Then we will feel the consequence of suffering or happiness. Therefore, to gain access from the visible world to the invisible world is to contemplate the ten evils and ten virtues after we have tasted the bitter or sweet fruit. This is a very important channel (medium of communication).

Through this channel, *The Sūtra of Kṣitigarbha's Fundamental Vows* provides us with many convenient methods so that we can enter the invisible world from the visible.

For example, because we are petty-minded without wisdom, we often take appearances as if they were the truth and only care to pay attention to concrete people, events and things. Therefore, Kṣitigarbha Bodhisattva Mahāsattva complies with our wish and suggests that we create statues of the Buddhas and Bodhisattvas to whom we can pay tribute and make offerings as well as care and provide for the Buddha's stūpas, temples, pagodas and all activities related to the Three Jewels.

He also suggests that we chant the Buddhas' and Bodhisattvas' names and study and read aloud *The Sūtra of Kṣitigarbha's Fundamental Vows* as convenient, speedy methods to help us contemplate and envision the merits, virtuous deeds and blessings of the Buddhas and Bodhisattvas, so that we can bravely and

 The Sutra of Ksitigarbha's Fundamental Vows

honestly make repentance to disclose the ten evil deeds that we have committed in order to bring us out of our immediate cowardice, fear, stress and impotence. In this way, our mind is expanded and elevated, and we are led and freed from the [bondage of the] visible world into the [spacious] invisible world.

The importance of this Sūtra is to help us open up the door of the invisible world; otherwise, we don't have any channel to reach into the invisible world.

Strictly speaking, we cannot say that we don't have any access to reach into the invisible world. In fact, we have many frequent and convenient paths to get there, especially to the lower parts of the invisible world. For example, our mentalities are often like that of hungry ghosts, animals and hell beings, only we fail to realize, acknowledge and be aware of how it happened until we have suffered severe pain and agony and felt the excruciating pain of "climbing a mountain of swords and sizzling in a caldron of burning oil". Only then do we realize that we have fallen into hell.

We often enter the lower parts of the invisible world without knowing how we traveled onto the path. This is a dangerous situation. *The Sūtra of Kṣitigarbha's Fundamental Vows* exerts severe warnings about the presence of the invisible world which we urgently need to recognize, but have failed to do so.

7. Advice at the Times of Birth and Death.

Since we are often so oblivious to our frequent travels into the invisible world, especially at the times of *birth and death*, Kṣitigarbha Bodhisattva Mahāsattva and those Ghost Kings clearly provide us with very practical advice:

Do not indulge in mourning or celebrating, worshipping ghosts and gods or offending them. The only thing that we can do is to forsake all beloved objects, money and wealth to praise, chant and make offerings to Kṣitigarbha Bodhisattva Mahāsattva and all the Buddhas and Bodhisattvas, as well as carry out Buddhist services such as participating in and supporting Buddhist establishments and activities. This is the best and most positive communication with the invisible world during the times of birth and death.

8. The Principle of Giving: Nobility should care for the Indigent while Commoners should make offerings to the Three Jewels.

For kings, high ranking officers, nobility and worldly leaders, the Sūtra states that if they can humbly give alms to sentient beings, their merits will be much greater than if they make offerings to the Three Jewels. For commoners who have little wealth and strength, offerings to the Three Jewels carry greater merits than almsgiving.

9. Kṣitigarbha Bodhisattva Mahāsattva is the Prime Representative of all the Buddhas, Dharma and Saṃgha in the Ten Directions.

At the dharma assembly in Trāyastriṃśa, not only does Bhagavat earnestly entrust Kṣitigarbha Bodhisattva Mahāsattva with the mission to rescue obstinate, hard-to-tame, habitual evildoing, sinful, suffering beings like us, but all the Buddhas and Bodhisattvas in the ten directions also jointly deputize Him with this mission. Kṣitigarbha Bodhisattva Mahāsattva also repeatedly responds with solemn vows to ease their worries.

    The Sutra of Ksitigarbha's Fundamental Vows

Here we must clearly recognize the merits of Kṣitigarbha Bodhisattva Mahāsattva. Why is He alone unanimously entrusted by all the Buddhas and celestial Bodhisattvas in the ten directions with the mission to be the prime representative of all the Buddhas, Dharma and Saṃgha in the ten directions?

First of all, His profound grand vow is inconceivable. Secondly, He has inconceivable miraculous power, inconceivable kindness and mercy, inconceivable wisdom, inconceivable eloquence and inconceivable convenient ways to rescue those seeking His help. With these infinite merits, Kṣitigarbha Bodhisattva becomes the *only rescuer* of us obstinate, hard-to-tame, habitual evildoing, sinful, suffering beings in Jambudvīpa during this Dharma-Declining Period. We must firmly keep this point in mind as we read and study *The Sūtra of Kṣitigarbha's Fundamental Vows*.

10. *The Sūtra of Kṣitigarbha's Fundamental Vows* is the Most Important Sūtra for all sentient beings of this era and this earth to make Direct Connections with Kṣitigarbha Bodhisattva Mahāsattva.

Each Buddha and Bodhisattva has His own special, superb method of cultivation that calls for specific prerequisites with certain "thresholds" to pass, and most methods are designed for virtuous men and virtuous women who have already made the vow of realizing *Anuttara-samyak-saṃbodhi*. Only they are qualified to practice these methods.

Right now, we cannot even rescue ourselves, nor pull ourselves out of the path of ten evil deeds and eight sufferings; therefore, all these exquisite cultivation methods are beyond our reach. Only Kṣitigarbha Bodhisattva sets no threshold and no prerequisite.

As long as we are willing to send the SOS signal and are willing to be rescued by Him, He will save us!

Therefore, Kṣitigarbha Bodhisattva Mahāsattva is especially meant to rescue, respond and safeguard us—beings with little faith and shallow virtue who are obstinate, hard-to-tame, habitual evildoing, sinful and suffering. Once we make a connection with Kṣitigarbha Bodhisattva Mahāsattva, we will receive His miraculous empowerment, protection and blessings and furthermore, receive and sustain all kinds of superb, convenient "Ksitigarbha Dharma-Doors-to-Enlightenment" (methods of cultivation).

Through these dharma-doors-to-enlightenment, it will be very easy to make a connection with all the Buddhas and Bodhisattvas and all kinds of superb dharma-doors-to-enlightenment. Therefore, we must diligently learn and study *The Sūtra of Kṣitigarbha's Fundamental Vows*.

Buddhist Glossary

▶ **Abundant-Jewels** (*Prabhūta-ratna*) **Tathāgata** In Sanskrit, *prabhūta* is "abundant"; *ratna* is "gem", "jewel" or "anything valuable or best of its kind". This name refers to a Buddha whose most distinct merit is to enable all sentient beings to have the abundant and superb treasures of the Buddha-dharma.

Ajita (Skt.) Invincible, unconquerable and irresistible. Another name for Maitreya Bodhisattva Mahāsattva, the next Buddha. See *Maitreya*.

All-Wisdom-Accomplished (*Sarvajña-siddhārtha*) **Tathāgata** In Sanskrit, *sarvajña* is "omniscient"; *siddhārtha* is "one who has accomplished his goal".

alienating speech Refers to speech, gossip or any negative talk that will cause disharmony among two or more people or within and between groups, nations, etc.

Amitābha Buddha (Skt.) Also known as *Amitāyus Buddha*. *Amita* means "infinite"; *abha* means "light"; *ayus* means "life". Therefore, He is also known as the Buddha of Infinite Light and Life. In this Buddha's world of Pure Land, there are no women and sentient beings of the lower three paths. There are only men, śrāvakas, pratyeka-buddhas, bodhisattvas and the Buddha.

anuttara-samyak-saṃbodhi (Skt.) Unsurpassed, perfect and complete enlightenment. Refers to unexcelled, correct and complete awareness, the perfect wisdom of a Buddha. *Anuttara* means "highest" or "supreme"; *samyak* means "perfect, true, proper"; *sambodhi* means "complete enlightenment". Such enlightened wisdom means one has the correct view and cognition of how each being feels and why the being thinks, speaks and acts the way he does in the past, present and future.

arhat (Skt.) One who is worthy. *Arhat* is the final of the four stages of fruition in *Hīnayāna* practice—*srotāpanna, sakṛdāgāmin, anāgāmin* and *arhat*. Each stage has its own specific measure of accomplishment. An Arhat is one who has destroyed the taints and fetters of "being" (existence), laid down the burden and attained the wisdom to understand the Four Noble Truths and is thus freed from all mundane troubles, afflictions and attachments, which eventually leads to being freed from rebirth in the Three Realms (the cycle of birth-death), ultimately validating the Arhat's nirvāṇa. Broadly speaking, Arhat is the highest stage of attainment for both *Hīnayāna* and *Mahāyāna*. While the goal for a Hīnayāna Arhat is individual deliverance, the goal of the Mahāyāna Arhat, one of the ten meritorious designations of the Buddha, is the deliverance of oneself and all sentient beings.

ārya (Skt.) Noble, excellent or venerable.

asaṃkhyeya (Skt.) Innumerable. See *numerical units.*

attributing the merits A conceptual process of sharing the blessings and benefits with other beings. It is one of the most important practices in Mahāyāna Buddhism. The purpose of it is to expand our mind by including others in our consideration and breaking the barriers that separate "I" from all other people, beings and the Buddhas. Buddhism believes that all beings in the ten dharma realms share the same mind, thus there should not be any self-centered segregation among all beings. It is also the best way to accumulate "capital" to become enlightened.

Authentic Teachings of *Tathāgata* or *Tathāgata*'s Authentic Dharma Refers to the following four basic dharma:

1. Four Dharma Seals;
2. Four Noble Truths;
3. Twelve Links of Dependent Origination—Leading to Existence; and
4. Thirty-Seven Aids on the Path of Bodhi: the practices of the Four Establishments of Mindfulness, Four Essential Exertions, Four Steps in Dhyāna Leading to Miraculous Power, Five (Virtuous) Roots, Five (Virtuous) Strengths, Seven Factors of Awakening and the Noble Eightfold Path.

Avalokiteśvara Bodhisattva Mahāsattva (Skt.) *Avalokiteśvara* refers to either "Lord Who Gazes Down (at the World)" or "He Who Hears the Sounds (Outcries) of the World". Depending on how the Sanskrit is translated, *avalokita* means "to look downward" and *īśvara* means "lord"; *loka* means "world" and *svara* means "sound, noise or voice". This Mahāsattva is from Amitābha Buddha's Pure Land, most distinguished for His great mercy. He also has a deep, intimate connection with sentient beings in Jambudvīpa and listens and answers to their sufferings prevalently. *Avalokiteśvara* is greatly venerated universally and also known as Bodhisattva of Compassion, Goddess of Mercy, Guanyin (China), Chenrezik (Tibet), Kannon (Japan) and Lokesvara (Thailand and Cambodia).

                    The Sutra of Ksitigarbha's Fundamental Vows

Avīci **Hell** (Unremitting Hell) In Sanskrit, *avīci* means "waveless"; also translated as "incessant". It refers to "never-ceasing hell", the lowest level of the hell realm with the most extreme suffering and most difficult to get out of. Sentient beings who have committed the most grave evil deeds are born here. Details are described in Ch. 3 of this sūtra. See *Unremitting Hell.*

> **Banner-of-a-Monk's-Robe** (*Kāṣāya-dhvaja*) **Tathāgata** In Sanskrit, *kāṣāya* refers to a monk's robe; *dhvaja* is "banner" or "flag". This name refers to a Buddha who upholds the banner of "being a monk in a monk's robe" signifying deliverance in the mundane world. It is a metaphor for being victorious in taming demons and foes that are in one's mind. Being a monk signifies the excellent merits of leaving the mundane way of living and becoming part of the saṃgha to pursue the ultimate enlightenment as a Buddha.

Bhadra Kalpa (Skt.) Auspicious Kalpa or Kalpa of Sages, name of the present kalpa. *Bhadra* means "auspicious, prosperous, praiseworthy and good (virtuous)". Each kalpa has 1,000 Buddhas who make their presence known. Śākyamuni is the 4th Buddha of this kalpa, and Maitreya Bodhisattva Mahāsattva (*Ajita*) will be the next Buddha.

Bhagavat (Skt.) Holy, venerable and revered. One of the ten meritorious designations of the Buddha used as a respectful address referring to "one who is the most honored, respected and glorious being of the past, present and future". *Bhaga* means "quality" and *vat* indicates its possession—"the one who possesses qualities". *Bhaga* can also mean "to crush" with *vat* indicating the ability—"one who can crush desire, hatred and delusional foolishness".

bhikṣu or *bhikṣuṇī* (Skt.) Literally, male or female beggar. Refers to a monk or nun who has joined the saṃgha and renounced all mundane possessions, passions and mission to cultivate the mind of Bodhi.

bodhi (Skt.) Awakening or enlightenment. Refers to the perfect wisdom, having understood, the way, and the truth. It denotes the wisdom of ending all delusions and afflictions and the realization of nirvāṇa. The bodhi of a Buddha is the ultimate, unsurpassed wisdom and is thus called *anuttara-samyak-saṃbodhi*: unsurpassed, perfect and complete enlightenment. One can achieve enlightenment through cultivation of the Three Vehicles—*Hīnayāna* (Small), *Pratyeka-buddhayāna* or *Madhyamayāna* (Middle) and *Mahāyāna* (Great).

bodhisattva (Skt.) An enlightened being. *Bodhi* means "enlightenment"; *sattva* is "sentient being". *Bodhisattvas* are enlightened beings who work on the mutual cultivation towards enlightenment of all beings.

Bodhisattva Mahāsattva (Skt.) A great enlightened being. *Mahā* means "great"; *sattva* means "being". When a sentient being has reached the 6th stage on the Path of Bodhisattva, the designation Bodhisattva Mahāsattva (or only Mahāsattva by itself) is used. There are ten stages on the Path before a bodhisattva validates the status of a Buddha.

Boundless-Body (*Anantakāya*) ***Tathāgata*** In Sanskrit, *ananta* means "boundless"; *kāya* means "body". Refers to a Buddha whose body is infinite without boundaries. A body without boundaries is hard for us to imagine, let alone to sculpt or paint. Contemplating *Anantakāya*'s image gives us the opportunity to break through our sensory limitations and lead us into the realm of the infinite, invisible world.

brahmacārī or *brahmacārin* (Skt.) An ascetic practitioner.

brahman (Skt.) Highest and most respected social caste in ancient India, superior to political and military leaders. Their main responsibilities were to make communications with the invisible world and give advice to the *kṣatriyas*. The society in ancient India was divided into four castes. The top elite caste was *brahman*, the educated, academic and religious. The second caste was *kṣatriya*, royalty and civil or military officers. The third caste was *vaiśya*, merchants and farmers. The fourth caste was *śūdra*, servants and slaves.

brahmarāja (Skt.) The king of a Brahmā heaven in the celestial realm. Also known as Lord Brahmā.

Buddha (Skt.) Literally, "enlightened" or "awakened". A sentient being who has validated all ten stages of the Path of Bodhisattva and reached full enlightenment is called a Buddha, the "Enlightened One". Only as a Buddha can one reach nirvāṇa. Śākyamuni is the Buddha who appeared in this civilization. He is the 4th Buddha in this current Bhadra Kalpa (Kalpa of Sages).

Burning Three Realms See *Three Realms*.

▶ *cakravartī* or *cakravartin* (Skt.) Wheel-turning king. *Cakra* means wheel; *vartin* means turning. See *wheel-turning king*.

  The Sutra of Kṣitigarbha's Fundamental Vows

cause-stage Refers to the time when a seed or cause was planted so as to receive desired results later.

celestial (*deva*) realm One of the six paths in the Sahā World, composed of 28 heavens: 6 in the *Realm of Desire*, 18 in the *Realm of Form* and 4 in the *Realm of Formlessness*. See *Sahā World* map.

chanting the name of a *Buddha* or *Bodhisattva* A Buddhist practice that brings infinite benefits. 1. Because the names represent their merits, contemplating their names will take our mind away from evil thoughts and bring us closer to virtue. 2. Chanting is a form of communication to make us closely connected with a Buddha or Bodhisattva. 3. Once we have formed a good habit of frequent chanting and contemplation of the name of a Buddha or Bodhisattva, when we run into a desperate situation, we can call out His name like a reflex to be swiftly rescued. 4. At the time of death when most sentient beings are in pain, agony, confusion and shock, the good habit of chanting will help the person receive salvation, guidance and protection, so the path of rebirth can be guided and uplifted.

collective *karma*-field In any place or circumstance where two or more people start interacting with a shared goal or interest, collective invisible forces are formed and can influence the participants' behaviors, such as in a family, on a battlefield, in a casino, on social media, on a football field, amidst a group, a society, or even a nation.

Conveniences of *Tathāgata* or *Tathāgata*'s Convenient Techniques Refers to the *Ten Pāramitās* or the ten stages of a bodhisattva to become a Buddha—the *Six Pāramitās* plus the *Four Infinite Minds* of Kindness (*maitrī*), Mercy (*karuṇā*), Joyfulness (*muditā*) and Renouncing (*upekṣā*).

cosmic world See *three thousandfold great cosmic worlds*.

▶ *dāna* (Skt.) Almsgiving, letting go or forsaking. There are three kinds of dāna—*dāna of alms* refers to monetary donation; *dāna of service* refers to personally getting involved in worthy causes and being of service; *dāna of dharma* refers to studying, practicing and validating the teachings of the Buddha while helping others to do the same. Each kind of dāna brings different levels of benefits. In Buddhist cultivation, *dāna* is often paired with another word, *pāramitā*. *Pāramitā* means to "reach the other shore", referring to the shore of ultimate deliverance. Cultivating *Dāna Pāramitā* or any other pāramitā alone will allow the practitioner to attain deliverance. See *Six Pāramitās*.

dānapati (Skt.) Generous donor and strong supporter of Buddhist matters.

deva (Skt.) A heavenly or celestial being. See *Eight Legions*.

devarāja (Skt.) A celestial king.

deeds (*karma*) There are three categories: 1. body/action; 2. mouth/speech; and 3. mind/thought. Only a deed that is free of greed and stinginess, hatred and jealousy, and arrogance with erroneous views (the deeds of the mind) is without karmic effect. See *virtuous and evil deeds*.

dharma (Skt.) A general term for any thing or phenomenon such as an event, attribute, being or existence. Also refers to the teachings of the Buddha on the absolute truth, virtue, law, causes and consequences. It is about how everything, including sentient beings, comes into being (into the visible world) and disappears again (into the invisible world). In the mundane world, any law, rule, regulation, guideline or "entity" is also considered a dharma.

dharma-**clouds** Refer to miraculous merits of the Buddha who can transmit His dharma through "clouds" which can only be perceived by the mind. These clouds can universally cover and shield all sentient beings, provide peace and refuge, and illuminate our minds with wisdom.

dharma-**door-to-enlightenment** or *dharma* **entrance** (*dharma-paryāya*) Refers to convenient means and effective ways of practice as instructed in the sūtras which will lead to further enlightenment. Examples include burning incense, paying homage to the images of the Buddhas and Bodhisattvas, chanting their names, reading sūtras, learning the dharma and sūtras, and so forth.

dharma **king** Refers to a Buddha who, with his unsurpassed wisdom, knows all the dharma. Thus, he is the mentor, role model, teacher and rescuer of all sentient beings.

Dharma **of No-Birth** The merit and capacity of a bodhisattva who has passed the 6th stage among a total of ten stages (on the Path of Bodhisattva). At the 7th, 8th and 9th stages, a bodhisattva has gained insight and penetrated deeply into the true nature of existence with non-dualistic wisdom and validated that all existences have no beginning and no end (or are non-arisen and non-destroyed). Hence,

  The Sutra of Ksitigarbha's Fundamental Vows

his endurance capacity of mind enters directly into the elimination of controversy and absence of obstacles, thus continuing to realize the truthful realm of all phenomena and dwelling in it with no-regression.

***Dharma* (Law) of Suffering and Happiness** There are two points of importance. First is to know the true meaning of suffering (impotence about the Eight Sufferings) and happiness (departing from one's ten evils) as taught by the Buddha. Second is that only after learning about the Truth of Suffering (First Noble Truth), can one have the momentum to seek true happiness. "Law" is *dharma* in Buddhism.

***Dharma* (Law) of Cause and Consequence** Also known as the law of causality—the universal law of how all phenomena interrelate and come into being. It consists of four stages: cause, condition, consequence and retribution.

The *cause* as a "seed" always starts from the deeds of the mind. Then it gathers favorable or unfavorable *conditions* as the seed is being nurtured to sprout and gradually grows into a tree. When the conditions are mature, it will bear fruits—the *consequence* (happiness or suffering). As our mind never stops working, further deeds react to the consequence which is the *retribution* (to the previous cause, condition and consequence). And then, this retribution becomes the cause of the next cycle of causality. As the time span of the maturity varies, the appearance of the consequence can take more than one lifespan—i.e. one or more rebirths—which constitutes the cycle of existence (*samsāra*).

With regards to sentient beings, what is experienced in the present is a consequence of causes planted through present and past deeds of action, speech and thought (mind). Present deeds of action, speech and thought are causes that will lead to consequences which will be experienced in the present and future. Virtuous deeds lead to happiness, while evil deeds lead to suffering.

***dharma* realms** Also known as "ten dharma realms", the realms of the Buddhas, bodhisattvas, pratyeka-buddhas, arhats, celestial beings (devas), asuras (which can appear in the celestial realm as well as in any of the following four realms), humans, hungry ghosts, animals and hell beings.

***Dharma*-Resemblance Period** The 2nd of the four dharma periods. See *Four Dharma Periods*.

dharma-voices The sound of Truth, referring to miraculous merits of the Buddha who can transmit the dharma through "sound" which can only be perceived by the mind. They carry the teachings of profound dharma, mainly expounded by the Buddha or Bodhisattvas.

dhyāna (Skt.) Contemplation, absorption, abstract meditation, reflection. Refers to conducting mindful focused-penetrating contemplation to halt all major and minor evils as well as to cease all doubts towards the Three Jewels and the Ten Virtuous Disciplines. See *Six Pāramitās*.

divided-identical body (*vigraha*) The Buddhas and Mahāsattvas, such as Kṣitigarbha Bodhisattva, have the miraculous ability to divide into an infinite number of identical entities to rescue sentient beings. See Ch. 2 of this sūtra: "The Assembly of Divided-Identical Kṣitigarbha Bodhisattvas". *Vigraha* is a Sanskrit word meaning "division, body, extension, expansion or separate, i.e. individual form or figure".

Dṛḍha-pṛthivī-devatā (Skt.) See *God of Solid-Firm-Earth*.

➤ **Eight Legions** (*aṣṭasenā*) Also known as "the devas, nagas and others of the Eight Legions". They are: 1. *deva*, celestial being; 2. *nāga*, dragon; 3. *yakṣa*, malignant flesh devourer; 4. *gandharva*, ghost of fragrance and music; 5. *asura*, a contentious being often waging wars with Lord Śakra and his followers; 6. *garuḍa*, king of birds with golden wings who preys on old or sick dragons; 7. *kinnara*, mythical being of song and dance; and 8. *mahoraga*, boa-shaped demon. As minor gods and ghosts, their ultimate duty is to protect the Buddha-dharma and encourage Buddhist practitioners to advance on their path even though, at times, they have to appear vicious. *Aṣṭa* means "eight" and *senā* means "legion" or "army".

Eight Sufferings All sentient beings suffer these eight sufferings in the mundane world. They are: 1. birth and living; 2. aging; 3. ailing; 4. dying; 5. parting with the loved; 6. meeting with the hated; 7. unable to have wishes fulfilled; and 8. being in constant agitation.

evil deeds See the *Ten Evil Deeds*.

evil paths or **realms** Also known as the three evil paths or lower three paths. Refer to existence as hungry ghosts, animals or hell beings. See *Sahā World* map.

evil times Refers to the Dharma-Declining Period in the Sahā World, the physical world that we are currently in, where sentient beings' minds are dark, suffering is most severe and the world is filled with contention and disasters.

fast or **fasting**   Refers to the discipline of eating rather than simply abstaining from food. On fasting days, practitioners shall observe taking one meal a day before noontime, preferably vegetarian without pungent vegetables and alcohol. This observation is also to help lay Buddhists learn and emulate the practice of the saṃgha in the temple. Fasting days are related to the full moon, half-moon and new moon. They are the 1st, 8th, 14th, 15th, 18th, 23rd, 24th, 28th, 29th and the 30th days of each month of the lunar calendar according to *The Sūtra of Kṣitigarbha's Fundamental Vows.*

filial   Befitting a son or daughter, which is not thinking, speaking or acting negatively towards one's parents.

Five Contaminations (*pañca-kaṣāya*)   Describes the state of the Sahā World, revealing why sentient beings of this time and place suffer so prevalently. In Sanskrit, *pañca* is "five"; *kaṣāya* is "contamination".

1. *Contamination of Kalpa* (*kalpa*). The era we are in is contaminated, a troubled and chaotic time when no one is spared.

2. *Contamination of Views* (*dṛṣṭi*). Our views are contaminated, as we are unable to correctly cognize and understand ourself nor our objective reality.

3. *Contamination of Afflictions* (*kleśa*). Our worldly cares, desires and state of mind are contaminated, misdirected by our evil deeds (greed, hatred, arrogance), thus constantly engaging in contention, creating confusion, distress and suffering.

4. *Contamination of Beings* (*sattva*). We are obstinate, hard-to-tame, habitual evildoing, sinful, suffering beings, thus creating barriers to enlightenment.

5. *Contamination of Destiny* (*āyuḥ*). Because of the previous four characteristics, we lack a higher mission and a meaningful goal in life, which also results in a short lifespan.

Five (Grave) Unremitting Sins   1. Being unfilial to the extent of killing one's parents; 2. harming or killing a Buddha, slandering the Three

Jewels and being disrespectful of the Buddhist sūtras; 3. invading or harming resident practitioners, blemishing monks or nuns, indulging in and committing sexual misconduct in a saṃgha group, killing or hurting a monk or nun; 4. pretending to be a monk or nun, cheating lay Buddhists and violating the Buddhist disciplines; and 5. stealing from a saṃgha or taking even one trivial item without permission. Committing any of these sins will cause one to magnetize and fall into the evil state of Unremitting Hell where suffering is immense, endless and relentless. See *Avīci Hell*.

five paths See *Six Paths*.

Five Rebellious (Grave) Sins 1. Patricide; 2. matricide; 3. killing an Arhat; 4. intentionally shedding the blood of a Buddha; and 5. causing disharmony in the saṃgha. Committing any of these sins leads to rebirth in Unremitting Hell.

Five Signs of Decay The signs appear shortly before a celestial being's death: 1. clothing turned filthy; 2. flowers on crown of head wither; 3. sweating in armpits; 4. foul bodily odor; and 5. uneasiness with anxiety. Celestial beings do not necessarily go through aging and ailing, but they do go through the process of birth and dying. Unlike the vivid and slow aging and dying process in humans, with celestial beings, death can occur suddenly without forewarning, and the impact is so strong that it can create resentment or even hatred, which would be the cause of their reincarnating in evil realms.

five pungent vegetables Refer to vegetables that can cause bad breath or gas and disturb the peacefulness of the mind. Also, they are considered stimulants and trigger desires. If eaten raw, these herbs could incite anger or disputes; if eaten cooked, it could lead to sexual desire and passion. Therefore, practitioners always abstain from and lay Buddhists, during fasting days, avoid eating these vegetables. They include: garlic, onion, scallion, chives and leek (any onion family) as well as asafoetida (stinking gum) and rape (mustard family).

Four Celestial Kings Each dwell on a side of Mount Sumeru; their kingdoms are situated on the 1st level of the Realm of Desire. They are guardians of humans and their kingdoms; they also guard the Buddha-dharma and shield sentient beings from the harm of evil gods and ghosts. They and their subordinates travel extensively to inspect and respond to virtuous or evil behaviors of all sentient beings. Their titles are: 1. Northern King, *Vaiśravaṇa* "one who

  The Sutra of Ksitigarbha's Fundamental Vows

hears all and can bless with merits and is knowledgeable"; 2. Southern King, *Virūḍhaka* "one who promotes the growth of virtuous roots"; 3. Eastern King, *Dhṛtarāṣṭra* "one who upholds the realm"; and 4. Western King, *Virūpākṣa* "one with pure celestial eyes of broad vision to guard Jambudvīpa". Many temples in Asia depict them as warriors with ferocious features and place them at the entrance of temple halls as a symbol of protection. See *Sahā World* map.

Four *Dharma* Periods Describe our relationship with the Three Jewels (Buddha, Dharma and Saṃgha). The four periods (ages) are:

1. *Authentic-Dharma Period*. When sentient beings are virtuous and respect the truth, a Buddha will appear in the world.

2. *Dharma-Resemblance Period*. A time when sentient beings are less interested in the dharma; although the Buddha is no longer present in the world, the dharma still closely maintains its authenticity.

3. *Dharma-Declining Period*. When the dharma is perceived without its authenticity, but sūtras are still available.

4. *Dharma-Extinction Period*. A dark age when sentient beings have completely lost interest in the Buddha-dharma and the Dharma is unknown and lost without sūtras and true practitioners.

Four *Dharma* Seals They are verified Truths: impermanence (*anitya*), suffering (*duḥkha*), lack of fixed characteristics (*anātman*: "non-self", i.e. lack of a fixed "I" or identity) and *nirvāṇa*. Also refers to: 1. everything conditioned is impermanent; 2. everything influenced by delusion is suffering; 3. all phenomena are empty and devoid of self; 4. nirvāṇa is true peace beyond extremes.

Four (Grave) Prohibitions Refer to staying away from the following deeds: 1. killing; 2. stealing; 3. sexual misconduct; and 4. deception, including untruthful speech or telling lies. The Buddha revealed to us about these four grave, evil deeds so that we could avoid the grave, evil consequences. Since ancient times, mankind has undisputedly shared the common view that these four deeds are to be prohibited or avoided in order to regulate our mind, behavior and social order.

Four Noble Truths The first and basic teaching the Buddha gave after His full enlightenment: 1. noble truth of *suffering*; 2. noble truth of *magnetization*, how suffering was aggregated; 3. noble truth of *cessation*, to cease the suffering; and 4. noble truth of the *path*, to be freed from the sufferings.

Four Unhindered Wisdoms   1. The unhindered wisdom of knowing all profound dharma; 2. unhindered wisdom of understanding the infinite meaning of all dharma; 3. unhindered wisdom of mastering different languages and forms of expression to aptly expound the dharma; and 4. unhindered wisdom of joyfully and tirelessly advocating the dharma according to one's readiness or request.

➤ *gāthā* (Skt.) Song, verse or stanza. An enriched form of dharma teaching that can be chanted or sung to practice mindfulness. This was a popular practice in ancient India.

ghosts and gods   Human beings are interconnected with ghosts and gods, especially lower-level evil ghosts and gods, according to each human's karmic deeds. The duties of ghosts and gods are to give "punishment" or blessings (i.e. not to confuse, disturb or ridicule) to humans according to each person's evil or virtuous deeds which in turn increases the ghosts and gods' strength towards virtue or evil. Therefore, ghosts and gods appreciate and are pleased to see humans performing virtuous deeds. Also, humans have more merits than lower-level evil ghosts and gods and usually don't encounter or mingle with them as they are meant to be kept in two separate realms. However, when one's mind is dark, troubled, ill or with heavy karma, one would attract them to induce unnecessary, evil entanglement.

ghost kings   Closely related with the well-being of humans and other sentient beings, overseeing matters and events (such as calamities, dangers, wealth, diseases, destinies, birthing, food and animals) along with their subordinates. They either bless or don't bless, depending on the being's virtuous or evil deeds; they do not punish.

Great ghost kings are in fact Bodhisattvas, even Mahāsattvas, who wear two hats with twofold tasks. Even if their appearances seem frightful or terrifying, they mean well and their hearts are kind and merciful—regardless of how they look, their only wish is for sentient beings to depart from evil deeds to gain benefits. Moreover, ghost kings discourage humans from worshipping them and their subordinates, urging us instead to praise and pay homage to the Three Jewels, the Buddha and Kṣitigarbha Bodhisattva to not only increase the ghost kings' virtuous strength but also for us humans to gain more capital to realize emancipation, as the ghost kings would do the same for themselves too. See Ch. 8 of this sūtra.

			The Sutra of Kṣitigarbha's Fundamental Vows

Ghost King of Destiny Among the many ghost kings, Ghost King of Destiny, also a Mahāsattva, is very important because he is in charge of life, from birth to death, and the well-being of all sentient beings. In Ch. 8 of this sūtra, he outlines the do's and don'ts that one should follow, in order to avoid misfortunes and gain happiness.

God of Solid-Firm-Earth (*Dṛḍha-pṛthivī-devatā*) In Sanskrit, *dṛḍha* is "firm, strong, unswerving, durable, reliable"; *pṛthivī* is "earth"; *devatā* is "god". It refers to the god of the great earth that nurtures and provides all the wealth that we need, such as crops, minerals and water; the earth also bears and supports all the establishments above and under the ground. This powerful god is one of the best representatives and a divided-identical body of Kṣitigarbha Bodhisattva Mahāsattva.

Great Eloquence (*Mahāpratibhāna*) Name of a Mahāsattva, referring to one with the merit of having great, convenient and enlightening speech. In Sanskrit, *mahā* is "great" and *pratibhāna* is "eloquence", "readiness of wit" and "presence of mind".

Great Iron-Enclosed Mountains (*Mahā-cakravāḍa*) An immense circular mountain wall that surrounds the four great continents and great salty oceans; also where all hells are located. In Sanskrit, *mahā* is "great"; *cakra* is "circle"; *vāḍa* is "enclosure". See *Hells & Karmic Seas* map.

Great Penetration Mountain King (*Mahābhijña-parvata-rāja*) **Tathāgata** In Sanskrit, *mahā* is "great"; *abhijña* is "higher knowledge" or "ubiquitous, supernatural wisdom-power", referring to penetrating wisdom; *parvata* is "mountain" (referring to Mount Sumeru), symbolizing karmic barriers and blockages; *rāja* is "king". This Buddha has the merits of penetrating and breaking down all barriers, making obstructions disappear. Without the barriers of the ten evil deeds, we can achieve true equality and supreme wisdom.

Hearer Also known as *śrāvaka*. Practitioners of the Small Vehicle (Hīnayāna) are called Hearers as they hear the dharma directly from the Buddha. See *Hīnayāna* and *Śrāvaka*.

heavens Refer to the celestial (*deva*) path, one of the six paths in the Sahā World. See *celestial realm*.

Heaven of Mastery over Others' Transformations (*Paranirmita-vaśa-vartin*) The highest celestial level of the six heavens in the Realm of Desire. *Deva Māra* (*Pāpīyān*) or "God" is in charge at this level, and not only does he have power to "create", he can also transform himself into other identities.

Heaven of Six Desires Covers six different levels of heavens where the sensory pleasures of the eyes, ears, nose, tongue and body (touch) are extraordinarily superb. In other words, the sight, sound, smell, taste and bodily sensations are truly beyond human imagination.

hell In Buddhism, hell is a "classroom" for auditory and visual education, not a place for punishment; it is not designed by a higher deity, but manifested by the sinful deeds of each being; and it's not permanent. It is a place where Kṣitigarbha Bodhisattva frequents to offer His salvation. The purpose of discussing the various hells is to warn sentient beings not to commit evil deeds so that they can avoid falling into those horrendous hells and also to urge them to see the necessity of being close to Kṣitigarbha Bodhisattva for His imminent rescue and of observing the ten virtuous disciplines. See *Hells & Karmic Seas* map.

Hīnayāna (Skt.) Small Vehicle, one of the three cultivation methods in Buddhism. *Hīna* means "lesser" or "inferior" and *yāna* means "vehicle". Small Vehicle practitioners are called Hearers or Śrāvakas, as they hear the dharma directly from the Buddha. The four stages of validation are *śrotāpanna, sakṛdāgāmin, anāgāmin* and *arhat*. The ultimate goal of Hīnayāna is to reach individual emancipation to become an Arhat. See *Three Vehicles*.

homage (*nama, namaḥ, namo*) To pay respect to, take refuge in, entrust to and be guided by the Buddha or Bodhisattvas to be led to ultimate enlightenment as well as to be blessed, protected and empowered by them. See *nama, namaḥ, namo* and *take homage in the Buddha*.

hungry ghost One of the three lower realms (paths). Being born in this realm is the ill consequence for stinginess and greed. Within this realm, there are several categories (sub-realms) according to the severities of the sins and each has different kinds of suffering. Hungry ghosts are tormented by constant, insatiable hunger and thirst—their necks are extremely thin, making everything hard to swallow, food is like burning lava rock and water is like fiery, scorching liquid. Hungry ghosts wander hopelessly in search of sensual fulfillment.

icchantika (Skt.) Those with great desire and destitute of Buddha-nature. Refers to one who: 1. disbelieves there is a new life after each death;

The Sutra of Ksitigarbha's Fundamental Vows

2. is not fearful of cause and consequence; 3. is unashamed and unrepentant; and 4. severs all virtuous roots.

ignorance (*avidyā*) In Buddhism, refers to a foolish, unenlightened mind, implying darkness of the mind without wisdom. Ignorance will cause one to go through endless reincarnations in the six realms of existence with continual suffering.

inexpressible One of the numerical units used in ancient India. Terms, from small to large, such as *nayuta, asaṃkhyeya*, inexpressible and inexpressible-inexpressible are commonly seen in Buddhist sūtras. See *numerical units.*

inner court of *Tuṣita* (in Tuṣita Heaven) Where Maitreya Bodhisattva Mahāsattva is currently expounding the dharma before reincarnating on earth as the next Buddha.

invisible, in-between entity Refers to the entity in the intermediate existence (*antarā-bhava*) between death and the following rebirth, lasting up to 49 days. In this state, there is no physical or visible body but the mind continues to function, seeking a new identity and new place to be reincarnated. This invisible, in-between state is similar to our dream state—when our physical body is not actively looking, listening, smelling, tasting, touching or moving, yet the dream is vividly "real". The entity in the invisible, in-between state (or the dream state) has supernatural powers across time and space.

▶ *Jambudvīpa* (Skt.) Name of the continent that we inhabit. Because it is situated south of Mount Sumeru, it is also called Southern Jambudvīpa. *Jambu* is the name of a tree said to abound in Jambudvīpa; *dvīpa* means continent. See *Sahā World* map.

▶ *kalpa* (Skt.) Refers to an immense measurement of time in ancient India. A small kalpa is represented as 16.8 billion years, and a mahā-kalpa as 1.3 trillion years. Within each kalpa, one thousand Buddhas make their presence known in the Sahā World.

karma (Skt.) Literally, "deed". See *deeds.*

Krakucchanda Buddha (Skt.) 4th of the "Seven Buddhas of Antiquity" as well as the 1st Buddha of the present kalpa—the Kalpa of Sages. His Sanskrit name refers to "firmly stop evil and act virtuously" as He has

the merit to lead sentient beings to know what is virtuous and what is
evil; what deeds are to be done and what deeds need to be avoided. In
other words, He is pure in upholding the ten virtuous disciplines.

kṣānti (Skt.) Receptivity, patience, forbearance or endurance. Refers to
expanding one's mind capacity through above-mentioned practices.
See *Six Pāramitās*.

kṣatriya (Skt.) Second highest caste in ancient India, comprised of kings
and royal family members as well as civil and military officers.
Brahmans were the most prestigious citizens, dominating religious
matters and knowledge. See *brahman*.

Kṣitigarbha Bodhisattva Mahāsattva (Skt.) *Kṣitigarbha* means "earth
treasury" or "earth store", which includes the underground treasures
and all growths and establishments above the ground; it also reflects
the hidden treasures in the minds of all sentient beings. *Kṣiti* is "earth"
and *garbha* is "womb". This Mahāsattva is most distinguished for His
grand vow to not become a Buddha until all beings, including those
in hell, are rescued and transformed. He is the best role model for all
Mahāyāna Buddhist practitioners as He demonstrates the importance
and indispensability of making grand vows which guide His course,
generate His strength and accomplish His deeds of rescuing all beings.
He can transform Himself to appear like a mirror image of the being
that He is to rescue; He can also create infinite divided-identical bodies
so as to rescue infinite sentient beings.

▶ **Lady *Māyā*** Refers to the Buddha Śākyamuni's mundane birth mother.
In Sanskrit, *māyā* means "illusion". Lady Māyā giving birth to Prince
Siddhārtha, who later became a Buddha, was a manifestation—the
truth is that Śākyamuni was already fully enlightened long before
He was born to Lady Māyā. He knew how to bring together all the
necessary elements in order to appear in this visible world, and He also
knew how to disintegrate these elements so as to fade into the invisible
world. Therefore, by being "born", He was only complying with the
"rules" of this mundane world.

Law of Cause and Consequence See *Dharma of Cause and Consequence*.

Law of Suffering and Happiness See *Dharma of Suffering and Happiness*.

lion's roar (*siṃhanāda*) Symbolizes leadership, might and fearlessness.

Lord *Brahmā* A brahmarāja, the king of a Brahmā heaven. Along with Lord Śakra, protects Buddhist practitioners and humans.

Lord of Land A subordinate of God of Solid-Firm-Earth, overseeing the well-being of sentient beings within a particular area or district.

Lord *Mahā-brahma* A *devarāja* in the celestial path who rules over the Brahmā worlds (the first dhyāna heavens) and is a Bodhisattva of the 8th or 9th stage. Along with Lord Śakra, he protects Buddhist practitioners and humans. See *Sahā World* map.

Lord *Śakra* King of Trāyastriṃśa Heaven and a Bodhisattva of the 3rd stage. Along with Lord Brahmā, he protects Buddhist practitioners and humans. Lord Śakra is often challenged by asuras. Also known as *Indra* ("lord"); *śakra* means "powerful, mighty, strong".

▶ ***Mahāsattva*** (Skt.) A great being. See *Bodhisattva Mahāsattva*.

Mahāyāna (Skt.) Great Vehicle, one of the three cultivation methods in Buddhism. *Mahā* is "great"; *yāna* is "vehicle". The Mahāyāna practice is the Path of Bodhisattva, and there are ten stages. The ultimate goal is to realize Buddhahood, complete enlightenment, through the deliverance of oneself and all sentient beings. See *Three Vehicles*.

Maitreya Bodhisattva Mahāsattva (Skt.) *Maitreya* means "benevolent" and "kind". He is destined to be the next Buddha. He also has another name, *Ajita*, and is now expounding the dharma in the inner court of Tuṣita Heaven. See *Ajita*.

Mañjuśrī Bodhisattva Mahāsattva (Skt.) *Mañjuśrī* means "gentle" or "sweet glory". He is considered the guardian of the Buddha-dharma known for his keen prajñā wisdom. It is said that all the Buddhas of the past, present and future derive their enlightenment from Him as their mentor. *Mañjuśrī* and *Samantabhadra* are the two Mahāsattvas often depicted on either side of Śākyamuni Buddha.

mundane blessings Can be categorized into three groups for humans: 1. blessings of good health, appearance and longevity; 2. blessings of wealth (visible and invisible such as intelligence and capability); and 3. blessings directed toward having a good mission/destiny in one's life which brings results in being successful in terms of family, career and social standing.

▶ *nāga* (Skt.) A dragon. See *Eight Legions*.

nama, **namaḥ** or **namo** (Skt.) Homage. For example, *namaḥ Kṣiti-garbhāya* means "homage to Kṣitigarbha"; *namo Buddhāya* means "homage to the Buddha". The difference in spelling depends on the first letter of the following word according to Sanskrit sandhi rules.

nayuta (Skt.) Myriad. Refers to a very large number. Some define as 100 billion, others as 100 million or 10 million. See *numerical units*.

Neither-Thinking-Nor-Not-Thinking Heaven The highest heaven in the Realm of Formlessness, which has four cultivation levels of samādhi. The Sanskrit name of this heaven is *Naiva-saṃjñā-nāsaṃjñāyatana*.

nirvāṇa (Skt.) A state of infinity validated through cultivation of Buddhism in which there is no suffering, birth or death, only eternal bliss.

No-Birth See *Dharma of No-Birth*.

no-outflow (*an-āśrava*) A mental state or wisdom of being away from the three poison fires of the mind (greed/stinginess, hatred/jealousy and arrogance with erroneous views), achieved through cultivation where one's action, speech and thought no longer bear any harmful effects that would cause a loss or leakage of blessings, virtues and merits.

non-human (*amanuṣya*) Generally refers to low-level ghosts and gods of the Eight Legions usually led by asuras. Their duties are to protect the Buddha-dharma and encourage Buddhist practitioners. *Amanuṣya* means "not human". See *Eight Legions*.

numerical units In ancient India, numeral terms from small to large—*nayuta, asaṃkhyeya*, unthinkable, indiscussable, inexpressible and inexpressible-inexpressible—are commonly seen in Buddhist sūtras. The "10 great numbers" described in the *Flower Ornament Sūtra* are as follows: *asaṃkhyeya* (numberless), boundless, infinite, unmatchable, uncountable, unspeakable, inconceivable, immeasurable, inexpressible and inexpressible-inexpressible.

▶ **obstinate, hard-to-tame, habitual evildoing, sinful, suffering being** The reasons for describing sentient beings of this time and on this earth as such are found throughout this sūtra. It is the kind and merciful teaching from the Buddha to call attention to all of us. Here are several key quotes to shed light on the description:

		The Sutra of Kṣitigarbha's Fundamental Vows

Ch. 2: "For those who still have the habit to do evil... I have been diligently exerting various techniques to rescue those most obstinate, hard-to-tame, sinful, suffering beings."

Ch. 6: "...whenever their minds generate an idea or take any action, the idea and action are all karmic and sinful deeds."

Ch. 7: "...as soon as a thought or an idea is instigated, their driving force is nothing but sin. Even if they have gained some temporary relief [from their sinful sufferings] along with a few benefits, soon after they will lose their original wish of seeking liberation. When they encounter unfavorable conditions, [they fall back into their habitual-sinful-karmic ways and let] evil thoughts grow one after another."

"These sentient beings who are habitually inclined toward evil will always make some petty evil suddenly grow into an infinite and enormous one."

Ch. 8: "...soon after those beings are liberated from the retributions of their sins, they fall back into the evil realms again."

"The temperaments of sentient beings of Southern Jambudvīpa are characterized by extreme stubbornness and unwillingness to yield. They are very difficult to mediate and tame."

Ch. 13: "Even if they have generated some benevolent mind and thoughts, a moment later they will regress from that virtue again. When encountering unfavorable conditions, their minds [will lean towards evil, and that is the time the evil thoughts] will grow and expand continuously."

➤ *pāramitā* (Skt.) "to reach the other shore" or "that which has gone beyond"; often translated as "perfection". Refers to reaching the shore of ultimate deliverance from the shore of suffering by sequentially cultivating each pāramitā while simultaneously cultivating the other nine pāramitās.

The ten pāramitās, also called the ten Conveniences of Tathāgata, are the ten stages on the Path of Bodhisattva—*dāna* (forsaking), *śīla* (observing disciplines), *kṣānti* (expanding endurance capacity of the mind), *vīrya* (diligently striving forward), *dhyāna* (mindful abstract contemplation), *prajñā* (wisdom of relinquishing dualistic views), *upāya* (expedient means), *praṇidhāna* (vow, profound meditation), *bala* (strength) and *jñāna* (strength of superb wisdom). The strength of the first *Six Pāramitās* can tame the roots of the six senses and such cultivation will carry a practitioner or a bodhisattva through various stages to the ultimate shore of liberation.

Paranirmita-vaśavartin (Skt.) See *Heaven of Mastery over Others' Transformations*.

Path of *Bodhisattva* The path of becoming a Buddha. There are ten stages and each stage cultivates one specific pāramitā, such as *dāna, śīla, kṣānti, vīrya, dhyāna* and *prajñā*. See *pāramitā*.

planting virtuous roots A term frequently used in Buddhism. It means once a seed is planted, roots and sprouts grow, which develop into a plant or a tree, bearing flowers and fruits that are beneficial and enjoyable. Doing virtuous deeds according to the Buddha's teachings sets virtuous roots which will bring about benefits in the future.

Pleasures of the Five Desires Refer to the five sensory pleasures—having beautiful scenes to satisfy the eyes, pleasant sounds to satisfy the ears, superb smells to please the nose, exquisite tastes to satisfy the tongue, and pleasing sensations to satisfy the body.

prajñā (Skt.) Wisdom or understanding. Refers to rising above the distinctions of "I" or one's ego to relinquish mundane, dualistic views—dwelling on two extreme ends, such as good or bad, large or small, existent or non-existent—and thus realizing the equal and universal wisdom in regards to all people, events and matters. *Prajñā* is realized through advanced cultivation of the Buddha-dharma. See *Six Pāramitās*.

pratyeka-buddha (Skt.) A cause-awakened and self-realized practitioner of the Middle Vehicle (*Madhyamayāna*) whose goal is to validate and break through the sequences of the "Twelve Links of Dependent Origination—Leading to Existence" revealing how everything, including all sentient beings, comes into existence and eventually goes into non-existence. *Pratyeka* is a Sanskrit word meaning "solitary" or "individual". See *Three Vehicles*.

Precious-Appearance (*Ratna-ketu*) *Tathāgata* In Sanskrit, *ratna* means "jewel, gem or anything valuable or best of its kind"; *ketu* means "bright appearance, form, shape, mark, symbol, flag or banner". This Buddha is most distinct for His superb appearance and overall image as a Buddha. In other words, His deeds of thinking, speech and action are excellent and stainless.

　　　　The Sutra of Kṣitigarbha's Fundamental Vows

Precious-Nature (*Ratna-maya*) ***Tathāgata*** In Sanskrit, *ratna* is "jewel, gem, or anything valuable or best of its kind"; *maya* is an affix used to indicate "made of" or "consisting of" and refers to "nature". This Buddha has the most distinct merit of treasuring the essence or nature of a Buddha. The precious nature of a Buddha is true permanence, true bliss, true self and true purity. Because of these characteristics, we can rely on, take refuge in and pay homage to this Buddha in order to bring out the same characteristics and qualities in us.

Pure Abodes (*Śuddhāvāsa*) In Sanskrit, *śuddha* means "pure"; *āvāsa* means "abode" or "dwelling". The Pure Abodes (fourth dhyāna) are the five highest heavens in the Realm of Form: Heaven of No Trouble (*Avṛha*), Heaven of No Heat (*Atapa*), Heaven of Virtuous Views (*Sudarśana*), Heaven of Virtuous Manifestations (*Sudṛśa*) and Ultimate Form Heaven (*A-kaniṣṭha*). See *Sahā World* map.

Pure-Moon (*Śuddha-candra*) **Buddha** In Sanskrit, *śuddha* is "pure", "stainless" and "clean"; *candra* means "moon" and "bright". Buddhist sūtras frequently use the moon to represent a state of purity, tranquility and a feeling of renewal, away from a sense of burning agitation or trouble.

Pure-Name King (*Vimalakīrti-rāja*) **Buddha** In Sanskrit, *vimala* is "pure, stainless"; *kīrti* is "fame, glory"; *rāja* is "king". This Tathāgata's merits is that he victoriously and successfully observes all disciplines without any impurity. Thus, he is designated as a king of purity.

➤ **realm** or **path** Refers to the state of existence of a certain category of beings. There are altogether ten realms: Buddhas, bodhisattvas, pratyeka-buddhas, arhats, celestial beings (devas), asuras (which can appear in the celestial realm or in any of the following four realms), humans, hungry ghosts, animals and hell beings.

Roaring-Lion (*Siṃhanāda*) ***Tathāgata*** In Sanskrit, *siṃha* means "lion" and *nāda* means "roar". This Buddha is like a roaring lion with his powerful and majestic voice, awakening sentient beings whose minds are in a delusional state.

root Refers to two kinds of roots: six sensory roots of the eyes, ears, nose, tongue, body, mind and "five virtuous roots".

1. *Sensory roots* are crucial faculties that we apply when interacting with the objective reality (the world). The harmony of these roots

indicates a person's mundane blessings which is the result of one's virtuous deeds. They are necessary tools while learning Buddhism.

2. *Five Virtuous Roots* are the roots of faith, diligent advancement, focused thought (on dharma), samādhi (Buddhist meditation) and wisdom. Once the roots are set in fertile soil (mind), they will grow and give strength of faith, strength of diligent advancement, strength of focused thought, strength of samādhi (meditation to elicit wisdom), and strength of wisdom.

sagehood Refers to one of the four levels of sagehood in *Hīnayāna* (Small Vehicle) as a śrotāpanna, sakṛdāgāmin, anāgāmin or arhat; or to a pratyeka-buddha of the *Madhyamayāna* (Middle Vehicle). See *Three Vehicles*.

Sahā **World** *Sahā* (Skt.) Enduring, bearing and suffering. The physical world we are currently living in is called Sahā World because sentient beings are muddle-minded and insensitive to suffering; thus, we are indifferent to seeking true deliverance, even though the world is filled with disasters and pain. However, it is also the best place and best time to achieve swift deliverance once people recognize the Three Jewels and learn the Buddha-dharma.

saintly stages The stages of cultivation on the Path of Bodhisattva from pre-Bodhisattva (prior to 1st stage) up through the ten stages on the Path of Bodhisattva (Great Vehicle) to become a Buddha.

Śakra (Skt.) See *Lord Śakra*.

Śākyamuni or *Shakyamuni* (Skt.) Name of the Buddha who appeared in this civilization. *Śākya* means "able, possible, practicable or capable" and is the name of His clan; *muni* means "sage". The word *Buddha* means "Enlightened One". Therefore, anyone who pursues the path of enlightenment by following Śākyamuni's teaching and footsteps can become a Buddha.

samādhi (Skt.) Concentration. A profound Buddhist meditation aiming to tame the roots of the six senses (eyes, ears, nose, tongue, body and mind)—especially our mind—thus eliciting great wisdom and the blessing to perform miracles.

Samādhi Self-at-Ease King (*Samādhīśvara-rāja*) A Bodhisattva Mahā-sattva. In Sanskrit, *samādhi* is "concentration"; *īśvara* is "powerful",

The Sutra of Ksitigarbha's Fundamental Vows

"able to", "capable of" or "master", referring to the mind being free from delusion; and *rāja* means "king".

Samantabhadra Bodhisattva Mahāsattva (Skt.) *Samantabhadra* means "universal worthy"—*samanta* is "universal", while *bhadra* is "worthy, blessed, auspicious, happy, prosperous and excellent". He is most distinguished for leading those practicing the Path of Bodhisattva and considered the patron of the *Flower Ornament Sūtra* (*Avataṃsaka Sūtra*). Along with *Mañjuśrī*, they are the two Mahāsattvas often depicted on either side of Śākyamuni Buddha.

Samantavipula (Skt.) Universal extensive. *Samanta* means "universal"; *vipula* means "extensive, broad, profound and abundant". This Bodhisattva was entrusted with the important task of circulating and advocating *The Sūtra of Kṣitigarbha's Fundamental Vows*.

saṃgha (Skt.) Assembly or multitude. Refers to a group of at least four monks or nuns who reside and practice together, observing the Ten Virtuous Disciplines and living by the "Six Points of Reverent Harmony" which refers to the practitioners' agreement and unity in action, speech and mind; observing the same disciplines; harmoniously upholding the Buddha's views; and equally sharing the dāna. Such unity will allow the saṃgha group to practice in harmony.

seed of bodhi Refers to "seed of enlightenment", which comes from the initial connection with the Three Jewels through hearing the names, seeing the images and knowing the merits of the Buddhas and Bodhisattvas.

sentient being (*sattva*) Refers to living beings with feeling and sentiment who perceive and respond with existing sensory roots, such as humans with their six roots of eyes, ears, nose, tongue, body and mind. There are six realms of sentient beings—celestial beings, humans, asuras, hungry ghosts, animals and hell beings. Each sentient being is born into one of these realms according to the virtuous or evil deeds that one has committed.

Seven Royal Jewels (*saptaratna*) Symbolize the virtues and blessings of a wheel-turning king whose seven attributes appear automatically and come in the form of: 1. golden wheel (*cakraratna*); 2. state elephant, 3. charger horse; 4. divine jewel (an octagonal gem so luminous it can light the path of his army by night); 5. queen; 6. treasury ministers (lay Buddhists); and 7. defense ministers (advisors and generals).

sexual misconduct One of the ten evil deeds defined by the Buddha as it will bring about harmful consequences and should be avoided. It refers to having sex out of wedlock and the retributions are having an unfaithful spouse and being foolish and ignorant.

śīla (Skt.) Virtue, nature, conduct and well-behaved. Refers to observing the disciplines (precepts) defined by the Buddha, such as the Ten Virtuous Disciplines. See *Six Pāramitās*.

Six *Pāramitās* The first six stages on the Path of Bodhisattva: the pāramitās of dāna, śīla, kṣānti, vīrya, dhyāna and prajñā. *Pāramitā* (Skt.) means to reach the shore of ultimate deliverance by departing from the shore of suffering through upholding and practicing the ten virtues and sequentially cultivating each pāramitā while simultaneously cultivating the other nine pāramitās. See also *pāramitā*.

1. *Dāna Pāramitā*. Making offerings and renouncing greed/stinginess, hatred/jealousy and arrogance with erroneous views until realizing the ultimate deliverance, as there are no regrets nor remnants of entanglement and attachment to the mundane world.

2. *Śīla Pāramitā*. Observing and keeping the ten virtuous disciplines until realizing the ultimate deliverance as one refrains from conducting any evil deeds.

3. *Kṣānti Pāramitā*. Expanding endurance and capacity of mind until realizing the ultimate deliverance. When encountering evil incidents, the mind can endure with virtuous capacity, as there is no vindictiveness.

4. *Vīrya Pāramitā*. Diligently striving forward and being zealous in cultivation until realizing the ultimate deliverance. When pursuing the Bodhi Path, one will neither slack off nor retrogress.

5. *Dhyāna Pāramitā*. Cultivating samādhi (mindful, penetrating contemplation which also refers to focus on absorption, abstract meditation and reflection) to halt all major and trivial evils to gain clear views as well as to cease all doubts towards the Buddha-dharma and travel far on the Path of Ten Virtuous Deeds until reaching the shore of ultimate deliverance.

6. *Prajñā Pāramitā*. Cultivating the wisdom of relinquishing dualistic views (dwelling on two extreme ends, such as good or bad, large or small, existent or non-existent) by rising above the distinctions of "I" or one's ego to realize the equal and universal wisdom in regards

     The Sutra of Kṣitigarbha's Fundamental Vows

to all people, events or matters until reaching the shore of ultimate deliverance.

six paths (realms) 1. Hell beings; 2. animals; 3. hungry ghosts; 4. humans; 5. celestial beings; and 6. asuras who are very contentious in nature and spread among the other five paths. Therefore, it is sometimes referred to as the "five paths".

Space Treasury (*Ākāśagarbha*) *Bodhisattva Mahāsattva* *Ākāśa* means "space"; *garbha* means "treasury". This Mahāsattva is a close partner of Kṣitigarbha (Earth Treasury) Bodhisattva as the livelihood of all sentient beings is intimately related with earth and space.

śramaṇa or *śramaṇikā* (Skt.) An ascetic and mendicant practitioner. Refers to a male or female Buddhist disciple admitted to monkhood (a monk or nun) who has left home to cultivate renouncing mundane possessions, passions and mission and has vowed to observe the disciplines of the saṃgha for the purpose of realizing Bodhi.

śrāvaka (Skt.) "One who listens" or "one who is hearing or listening to". Refers to a Small Vehicle (Hīnayāna) practitioner. Also known as a Hearer. See *Hīnayāna*.

śrotāpanna, sakṛdāgāmin, anāgāmin and *arhat* (Skt.) The four stages of fruition in Hīnayāna practice. Each stage has its own specific measure of accomplishment. The practitioner's ultimate goal is to become an Arhat. See *Arhat*.

stūpa (Skt.) Literally, "heap", referring to a burial mound containing the ashes or relics of an enlightened being. In Asia, a stūpa is often referred to as a pagoda.

Sumeru (Skt.) Wonderful, excellent, radiating. Name of a sacred, immense mountain often mentioned in Buddhist sūtras, located in the center of the four great continents. To the south of Mount Sumeru is the continent of Jambudvīpa; at its tip is Trāyastriṃśa Heaven. This mountain also symbolizes barriers and blockages between ourselves and other beings created by our evil deeds. See *Sahā World* map.

Superb Red-Lotus (*Padmottara*) *Tathāgata* The name *Padmottara* is a combination of *padma* and *uttara*. In Sanskrit, *padma* means "red lotus"; *uttara* means "superb" and "excellent". This Buddha realized complete Buddhahood like a red lotus growing out of a muddy swamp. The red lotus refers to complete enlightenment, and the swamp refers to the contentious, contaminated mundane world.

Padma also refers to one of the eight great frigid hells. Sinful beings fall into this red lotus hell as consequences of their evil deeds. There are open sores all over their frozen bodies that look like red lotuses which cannot be healed. This Tathāgata rescues and uplifts beings in Padma Hell who suffer these bodily wounds and leads them onto an auspicious, virtuous path according to their wish.

sūtra (Skt.) Literally, "thread". In Buddhism it means "discourse" (as a type of Buddhist sacred text) and refers to collections of the Buddha's teachings.

▶ **take homage in the *Buddha*** In Sanskrit, *Buddha* means the "Enlightened One". When we pay homage to a Buddha, it means that we honor, seek help and take refuge in wisdom. It also means that through the process of re-examining the experiences of our lives (i.e. our actions, speech and thoughts) as well as reflecting those of others back to ourselves according to the Buddha-dharma, we comprehend the causes of our suffering and happiness, our virtues and evils, and life's truths and falsities. The ultimate goal is to become a Buddha, with complete enlightened-wisdom and strength.

Tathāgata (Skt.) One who has come from the realm of truth. An honorable designation of a Buddha, indicating a fully enlightened being who embodies the fundamental truth of all transitory phenomena and has grasped the law of causality spanning past, present and future. *Tathāgata* also means "thus come one" indicating one who has arrived from the realm of truth or "thus gone one", indicating one who has gone to the world of enlightenment. For the ten other designations, see *Ten Meritorious Designations of Tathāgata*.

ten *dharma* realms See *dharma realms*.

ten directions Refer to the ten directions of space, i.e. the eight points of the compass—north, south, east, west, northeast, northwest, southeast, southwest—plus zenith (up) and nadir (down). Figuratively means "all directions" or "everywhere".

Ten Evil Deeds Deeds that cause harmful, harsh consequences: 1. killing, 2. stealing, and 3. sexual misconduct (three deeds of body/action); 4. deceptive speech (lying), 5. alienating speech, 6. ill-intended (harmful) speech, and 7. frivolous speech (four deeds of mouth/ speech); 8. greed/stinginess, 9. hatred/jealousy, and 10. arrogance with

    The Sutra of Ksitigarbha's Fundamental Vows

erroneous views (three deeds of mind/thought). Refer to *The Sūtra of the Path of Ten Virtuous Deeds*. See also *Ten Virtuous Disciplines*.

Ten Meritorious Designations of *Tathāgata* Also known as the ten characteristics or epithets of a Buddha.

1. *Arhat*. One who is worthy of offerings and who can reciprocate accordingly. See *Arhat*.

2. *Samyak-sambuddha*. One of perfect and complete enlightenment, correct and universal. *Samyak* is "perfect"; *sam* is "complete"; *buddha* is "enlightened one". The Buddha is one who is fully awakened with omniscient wisdom and understands that all dharma is truly indestructible (*abhedya*), i.e. complete deliverance, as well as immovable and permanent (*acala*), like a mountain.

3. *Vidyā-caraṇa-sampanna*. One who is fully endowed with (/accomplished in) understanding and conduct. *Vidyā* is "understanding, knowledge"; *caraṇa* is "conduct"; *sampanna* is "endowed with". The Buddha alone has realized the wisdom of knowing the history of all past beings and the moment of destruction of their impurities; he knows the future and present in the same way.

4. *Sugata*. One who is well-gone. *Su* is "good"; *gata* is "gone". The Buddha has surpassed all kinds of deep samādhi and boundless great wisdom.

5. *Lokavid*. One who is knower of the mundane world. *Loka* means "world"; *vid* means "to know". The Buddha is one who is enlightened and has resolved all entanglements and entrapments of the mundane world.

6. *Anuttara*. One who is unsurpassed. *Anuttara* means "supreme, incomparable, excellent, highest and best". The Buddha is without superior among all sentient beings as he has realized nirvāṇa—the highest dharma—all alone and leads/guides others to nirvāṇa. No one is as equal nor surpasses him in discipline, samādhi and wisdom.

7. *Puruṣa-damya-sārathi*. One who is the leader of the caravan of men to be tamed and converted. *Puruṣa* is "man"; *damya* means "to be tamed and trained" and *sārathi* is "leader and guide". The Buddha, with his great kindness and merciful wisdom, uses a voice sometimes sweet, sometimes harsh, sometimes warm, so that the caravan does not lose its way. He governs men by the three-fold path and never abandons anyone along the way.

8. *Śasta-deva-manuṣyāṇām*. One who is the most praiseworthy and excellent mentor of celestial beings and humans. *Śasta* is "praiseworthy, best, excellent"; *deva* is "celestial being"; *manuṣya* is "human being".

9. *Buddha*. "The Enlightened One", an awakened being who has realized perfect wisdom of the truth and thereby is liberated from all existence, and before his own attainment of nirvāṇa, reveals the method of obtaining it.

10. *Bhagavat*. One who is the most honored, respected and glorious being of the past, present and future. *Bhaga* means "quality" and *vat* indicates its possession—"the one who possesses qualities". *Bhaga* can also mean "to crush" with *vat* indicating the ability—"one who can crush desire, hatred and delusional foolishness".

Ten Virtuous Disciplines, Ten Disciplines or **Ten Virtues** Cultivating the ten virtuous disciplines (precepts) as defined by the Buddha results in beneficial blessings and leads to ultimate deliverance. All sentient beings are encouraged to refrain from committing the ten evil deeds in order to depart from suffering and gain happiness. Once we stay away from committing these harmful deeds, we are observing the ten virtuous disciplines and will thus gain the 71 benefits. Refer to *The Sūtra of the Path of Ten Virtuous Deeds*. See also *virtuous and evil deeds* and *Ten Evil Deeds*.

Thirty-Seven Aids on the Path of *Bodhi* (*saptatriṁśa-bodhipākṣika-dharma*) In Sanskrit, *saptatriṁśa* is "thirty-seven"; *bodhipākṣika* means "wings of awakening" (*bodhi* for "enlightenment", *pakṣa* for "wing" or "condition"); *dharma* refers to "factor". In many of the discourses, the Buddha referred to the significance of cultivating these 37 requisites, factors, qualities and conditions which would lead one to enlightenment. Presented in seven groupings, they are: the Four Establishments of Mindfulness, Four Essential Exertions, Four Steps in Dhyāna Leading to Miraculous Powers, Five (Virtuous) Roots, Five (Virtuous) Strengths, Seven Factors of Awakening and the Noble Eightfold Path.

Thirty-Three Heavens Also known as *Trāyastriṁśa* Heaven.

Three Jewels Refer to the Buddha, the Dharma and the Saṃgha.

Three Realms or **Worlds** (*Tri-dhātu* or *Tri-loka*), also known as the "Burning Three Realms", are the three levels of realms in the Sahā

   The Sutra of Ksitigarbha's Fundamental Vows

World. Sentient beings are born in one of these realms as consequences of their deeds:

1. Realm of Desire (*kāma-dhātu*), which includes the six heavens of desire, the human path, asura path and the lower three evil paths;

2. Realm of Form (*rūpa-dhātu*), a world of superb virtuous blessings without the confusion of desires; and

3. Realm of Formlessness (*ārūpya-dhātu*), a pure transcendent world without the presence of any form. See *Sahā World* map.

Although the upper realms are more blissful than the human realm, the bliss is not permanent, and the suffering of reincarnation will arrive like a house on fire.

The term "Burning Three Realms" originates in the *Lotus Sūtra*, Ch. 3. In this sūtra, the Buddha tells a metaphor about an elderly man trying to persuade his children to leave a run-down house that was on fire. But his children were so involved in their play that they were oblivious to the danger. Thus, the elder had to lure them out by telling them there were carriages of goat, deer and ox waiting for them outside, and he succeeded. What was actually waiting outside was a very splendid carriage pulled by a white ox. Symbolically, the Buddha is the elderly man, the goat, deer and ox are the Three Vehicles, the white ox is the supreme great Mahāyāna, we sentient beings are his children, and the burning house is the world we are in.

three thousandfold great cosmic worlds Refers to one Buddha land—a great universe. Also known as the three thousandfold world system, trichiliocosm or *tri-sāhasra mahā-sāhasra loka-dhātu*. In Sanskrit, *tri* is "three", *sāhasra* is "thousand", *mahā* is "great"; and *loka-dhātu* is "world-system", referring to a universe.

In Buddhist cosmology, there are infinite numbers of worlds. Each small world consists of a Mount Sumeru in the center, the surrounding seven rings of oceans and mountains, the four great continents—*Jambudvīpa* (south) where we live, *Uttara-kuru* (north), *Pūrva-videha* (east) and *Apara-godānīya* (west)—altogether encircled by the Great Iron-Enclosed Mountains. There is also a sun, moon, various celestial bodies and the first dhyana heavens.

One thousand such worlds plus the second dhyana heavens form a "small thousandfold world", a small universe. One thousand *small thousandfold worlds* plus the third dhyana heavens form a "medium thousandfold world", a medium universe. One thousand *medium thousandfold worlds* plus the fourth dhyana heavens and the Realm of Formlessness form a "great thousandfold world", or the three thousandfold great cosmic worlds, a great universe of a billion small worlds. In such a *great thousandfold world* a Buddha appears and guides beings to liberation. There are countless Buddha lands, and the Sahā World is one of these great universes. See *Sahā World* map.

Three Vehicles Refers to the three kinds of Buddhist cultivation: Small, Middle and Great Vehicles.

1. Small Vehicle or *Hīnayāna*. Practitioners are called Hearers (as they hear the dharma directly from the Buddha). The goal is to reach individual emancipation from the reincarnation cycle of birth and death. There are four stages: śrotāpanna, sakṛdāgāmin, anāgāmin and arhat. An accomplished practitioner is called an *Arhat*.

2. Middle Vehicle, *Madhyamayāna* or *Pratyekabuddhayāna*. The goal is to validate and break through the sequences of the "Twelve Links of Dependent Origination—Leading to Existence". An accomplished practitioner is called a *Pratyeka-buddha*.

3. Great Vehicle or *Mahāyāna*. One's deliverance comes from the deliverance of oneself as well as all sentient beings. The practitioner has to go through ten stages on the Path of Bodhisattva to reach the final goal—a *Buddha*. "Vehicle" in Sanskrit is *yāna*.

transformational entity (body) Refers to one of the Buddhas' and Bodhisattva Mahāsattvas' miraculous conveniences—the ability to appear in any form in order to save beings in the six realms of existence.

***Trāyastriṃśa* Heaven** *Trayas* means "three" and *triṃśa* means "thirty"; thus, *Trāyastriṃśa* Heaven is also called the Thirty-Three Heavens. It is situated on the top of Mount Sumeru and is the second level of the six heavens of the Realm of Desire. Lady Māyā, the Buddha's mundane mother who passed away seven days after giving birth to Prince Siddhārtha, was reincarnated in Trāyastriṃśa Heaven. Prince Siddhārtha later became Śākyamuni Buddha. See *Sahā World* map.

***Tuṣita* Heaven** (Heaven of Content and Knowledge) The inner court of *Tuṣita* (Skt.) is the place where Maitreya Bodhisattva Mahāsattva is currently expounding the dharma before reincarnating on earth as the next Buddha. Before the last rebirth to become a Buddha, all bodhisattvas reside in this inner court, including Śākyamuni Buddha.

Twelve Links of Dependent Origination—Leading to Existence The Sanskrit for "twelve links of dependent origination" is *dvādaśāṅga pratītyasamutpāda*. Also known as "twelve *nidānas*". It is the inter-linked factors of *saṃsāra* (reincarnation or cycle of existences). The process of the twelve links enables a seed of thought (ignorance) to arise from the invisible, through the inclination and manifestation of the mind, to the visible to appear as a sentient being, event or matter, step-by-step leading to aging and death (causing rebirth). This will lead back to ignorance and start the cycle all over again. All mundane existence or coming into being must perpetually go through these twelve links. They are mostly conceptual, and the process can be instant without conscious awareness. This dharma is also known as the Dharma of Birth and Death, the Dharma of Twelve Links of Causes and Conditions, and the Dharma of Karmic Force.

1. Ignorance (*avidyā*), also unenlightenment, illusion and delusion, leads to
2. action (*saṃskāra*), also activity i.e. fabrication, construction and conditioned phenomena, which leads to
3. discriminating consciousness (*vijñāna*), also discernment, i.e. initial cognition, which leads to
4. name and form (*nāmarūpa*), mind-and-body, i.e. the union of mental phenomena (name) and physical phenomena (form) that constitutes the five aggregates/*skandha*s, which leads to the
5. six roots or organs (*ṣaḍāyatana*) of the eyes, ears, nose, tongue, body and mind, i.e. the sense organs or the roots of sensation, which leads to
6. contact (*sparśa*), i.e. the interaction between the 6 roots, 6 dusts and 6 senses that manifests the 18 *dhātu* or realm of senses, which leads to
7. reception or sensation (*vedanā*), i.e. feeling, which leads to
8. craving (*tṛṣṇā*), also desire and thirst, which leads to
9. grasping (*upādāna*), i.e. clinging, which leads to
10. becoming (*bhava*), also being and existing, i.e. becoming into one of the 25 forms/realms of existence, which leads to
11. birth (*jāti*), which leads to
12. aging and death (*jarāmaraṇa*).

With these perpetual twelve links as the cause, it prevalently brings about confusion, worries, sorrow, grief, suffering, agitation and torment, even temporary pleasure, and concludes with the eight sufferings of all sentient beings in the mundane world.

> **Unremitting Hell** (*Avīci* Hell) The lowest level of the hell realm with the most extreme suffering and most difficult to get out of. Sentient beings who have committed the most grave evil deeds are born here. The suffering in this hell is experienced and perceived as:

1. no pause from unremitting sufferings;
2. no space as one's agony fills the entire place;
3. no intervals between various torturings;
4. no exemption to whoever has committed the evil deeds; and
5. no break from continuous deaths and rebirths.

unthinkable, indiscussable, immeasurable, unspeakable Numeral concepts in ancient India referring to immense numbers that are far beyond mundane numeral description. See *numerical units*.

upāsaka and *upāsikā* (Skt.) Male and female lay Buddhists who observe the Five Disciplines and are serious in their Buddhist practice. The Five Disciplines are: staying away from the deeds of killing, stealing, sexual misconduct, deceptive speech (lying) and alcohol.

upside-downness In Sanskrit is *viparyāya* and means "cognitive distortion, inverted, reverse or contrary to the truth". Refers to the fact that we always think, speak and act the opposite way of truly benefiting ourselves and in fact, contradicting the Truth—the Buddha's teachings.

> **vehicle** In Sanskrit is *yāna* as in *Mahāyāna* (Great Vehicle) or *Hīnayāna* (Small Vehicle). See *Three Vehicles*.

Vipaśyin Buddha (Skt.) *Vipaśyin* refers to "clear views of all kinds" and is the name of the 1st Buddha of the "Seven Buddhas of Antiquity". This Tathāgata has the merits of correct contemplation and observation without any barrier or interference. Chanting His name frequently will prevent us from falling into the three evil paths.

virtuous and **evil deeds** In Buddhism, the definition of *virtuous* is "beneficial with no harm"; the definition of *evil* is "harmful without benefit". There are ten evil deeds in three categories:

1. three deeds of *body/action*—killing, stealing, sexual misconduct;

2. four deeds of *mouth/speech*—deceptive speech (lying), alienating speech, ill-intended (harmful) speech, frivolous speech;

3. three deeds of *mind/thought*—greed/stinginess, hatred/jealousy, arrogance with erroneous views.

   The Sutra of Ksitigarbha's Fundamental Vows

What are virtuous deeds? Departing from these ten evil deeds is doing and practicing virtuous deeds. See *Ten Virtuous Disciplines*.

virtuous men or **virtuous women** Those who observe and uphold the Ten Virtuous Disciplines.

virtuous roots Refer to the Five Virtuous Roots of faith, diligent advancement, focused thought (on dharma), samādhi (Buddhist meditation) and wisdom. Once the roots are set in fertile soil (mind), they will grow and give strength of faith, strength of diligent advancement, strength of focused thought, strength of samādhi (meditation to elicit wisdom) and strength of wisdom.

vīrya (Skt.) Vigor or strength. Refers to advancing diligently and courageously in pursuing deliverance. See *Six Pāramitās*.

➤ **wheel-turning king** (*cakravartī*) A bodhisattva of the 2nd stage. In the mundane world, an influential and virtuous leader who possesses the blessings of the Seven Royal Jewels and the merits to lead and educate his people away from the ten evils with the guidance of the Ten Virtuous Disciplines.

Wonderful-Voice (*Mañjughoṣa*) **Buddha** In Sanskrit, *mañjughoṣa* means "having a sweet voice" and refers to a Buddha with merits of a most beautiful voice that can awaken those living in delusive dreams.

➤ *yakṣa* (Skt.) Literally, "speedy, courageous, strong". Refers to a malignant and violent being, a devourer (of human flesh) who dwells in the earth, air and the lower heavens. See *Eight Legions*.

Yamarāja (Skt.) King of *Suyāma* Heaven and controller of hells and their ghosts—thus, he has double identities and double responsibilities. *Yamarāja* informs and announces where newly deceased beings will reincarnate after reviewing the deeds these beings committed in their most recent lifetime. *Yama* means "double" (as in identical) or "twin" and also refers to equal and fairness as he treats all sentient beings equally and fairly, according to the severity of their sins, regardless of their previous identities or where they came from. *Rāja* is "king".

yojana (Skt.) An ancient Indian measure of distance. One *yojana* is about 10 kilometers or 6 miles.

MAP:
Relationship between
Sahā World, Three Realms and Six Paths

Three Realms
TRAYA-DHĀTAVAḤ

Realm of Formlessness
ĀRŪPYA-DHĀTU

FOUR HEAVENS:

I. Infinite Space
Ākāśānantyāyatana
(or Mahāmāheśvara)

II. Infinite Cognition
Vijñānānantyāyatana

FOUR DHYĀNA HEAVENS:

V. No Trouble
Avṛha

VI. No Heat
Atapa

VII. Virtuous Views
Su-darśana

Realm of Form
RŪPA-DHĀTU

DHYĀNA IV

I. Blissful Birth
Puṇya-prasava

II. Loving Blessings
An-abhraka

DHYĀNA III

I. Lesser Purity
Parītta-śubha

II. Infinite Purity
Apramāṇa-śubha

DHYĀNA II

I. Lesser Light
Parīttābha

II. Infinite Light
Apramāṇābha

DHYĀNA I

I. Multitudes of Brahmā
Brahma-kāyika

II. Ministers of Brahmā
Brahma-purohita

SIX HEAVENS:

III. Virtue and Wonder
Suyāma / Yāma

IV. Content and Knowledge
Tuṣita

MOUNT SUMERU

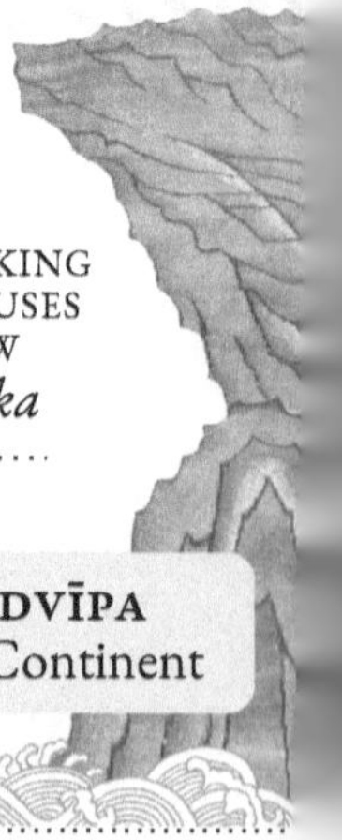

Realm of Desire
KĀMA-DHĀTU

I. Four Celestial Kings:
Catur-mahārāja-kāyika

MOON

EASTERN KING
HE WHO UPHOLDS THE REALM
Dhṛtarāṣṭra

SOUTHERN KING
HE WHO CAUSES TO GROW
Virūḍhaka

FOUR GREAT CONTINENTS

FOUR CONTINENTS OF HUMANS:
CATUR-DVĪPA

Eastern Continent of Superb Bodies
Pūrva-videha

JAMBUDVĪPA
Southern Continent

THREE EVIL PATHS:
APĀYA-BHŪMI

Hell
Naraka-gati

Animal
Tiryagyoni-gati

WE ARE HERE

Six Paths
ṢAḌGATI

III. Non-Existence
Ākiṃcanyāyatana

IV. Neither-Thinking-Nor-Not-Thinking
Naiva-saṃjñā-nāsaṃjñāyatana

VIII. Virtuous Manifestations
Su-dṛśa

IX. Ultimate Form
A-kaniṣṭha

III. Abundant Fruition
Bṛhat-phala

IV. No Thought
Asaṃjñi-sattva

III. Universal Purity
Śubha-kṛtsna

III. Light and Sound
Ābhāsvara

III. Great Brahmā
Mahā-brahma

Celestial Path
DEVA-GATI
(28 HEAVENS)

V. Joyful Transformations
Nirmāṇa-rati

VI. Mastery Over Others' Transformations
Paranirmita-vaśavartin

II. TRĀYASTRIṂŚA HEAVEN
Thirty-three Heavens

SUN

WESTERN KING
HE WHO SEES
ALL
Virūpākṣa

NORTHERN KING
HE WHO HEARS
ALL
Vaiśravaṇa

FOUR GREAT SALTY OCEANS

Western Continent
for Trading Cows
Apara-godānīya

Northern Continent
of Superb Place
Uttara-kuru

Human Path
MANUṢYA-GATI

Asura Path
ASURA-GATI
(can appear in any of
the five paths)

Hungry Ghost
Preta-gati

Three Evil Paths
APĀYA-BHŪMI

Sahā World
SAHĀ-LOKADHĀTU

Great Iron-Enclosed Mountains, Eighteen Major Hells and Three Karmic Seas

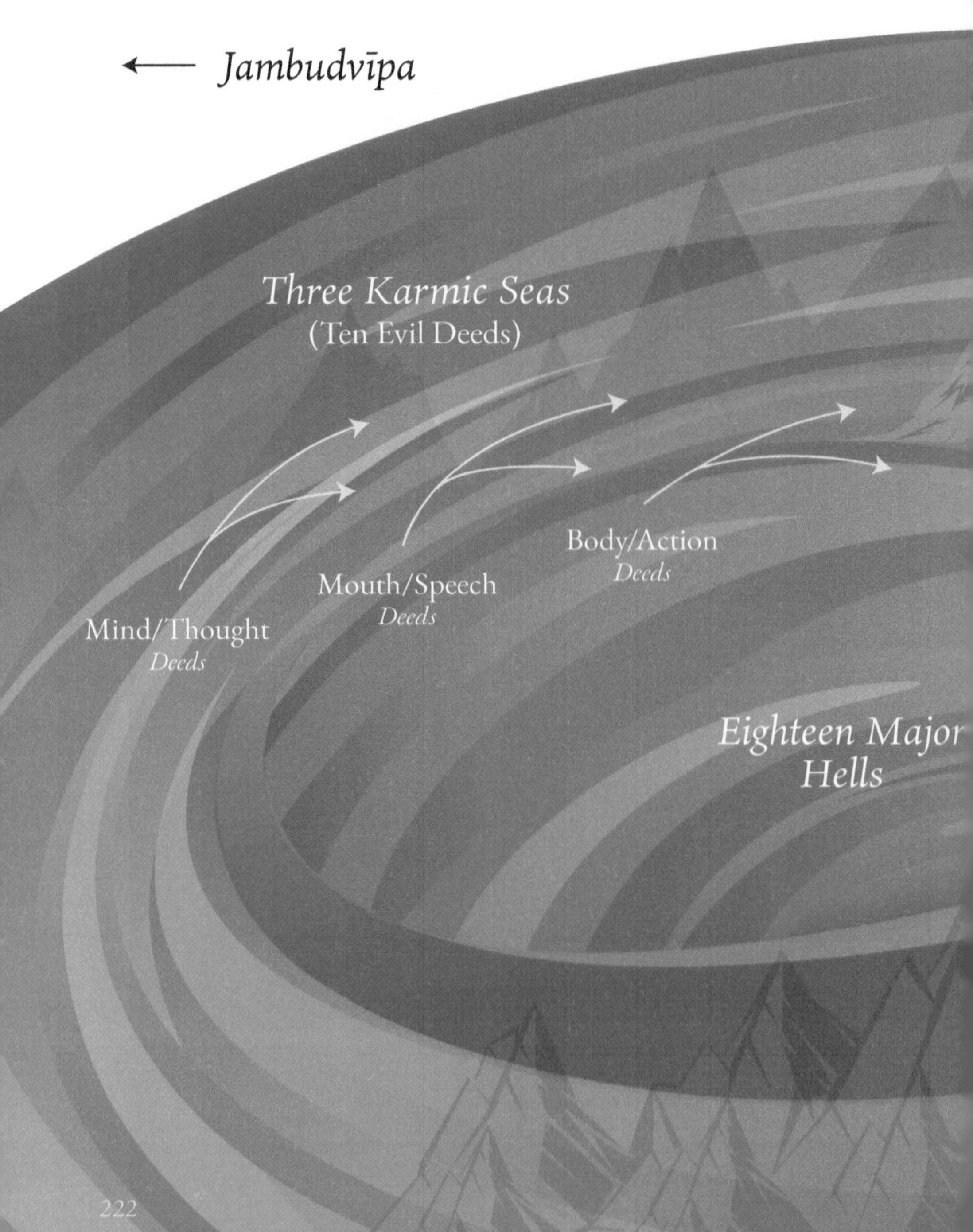

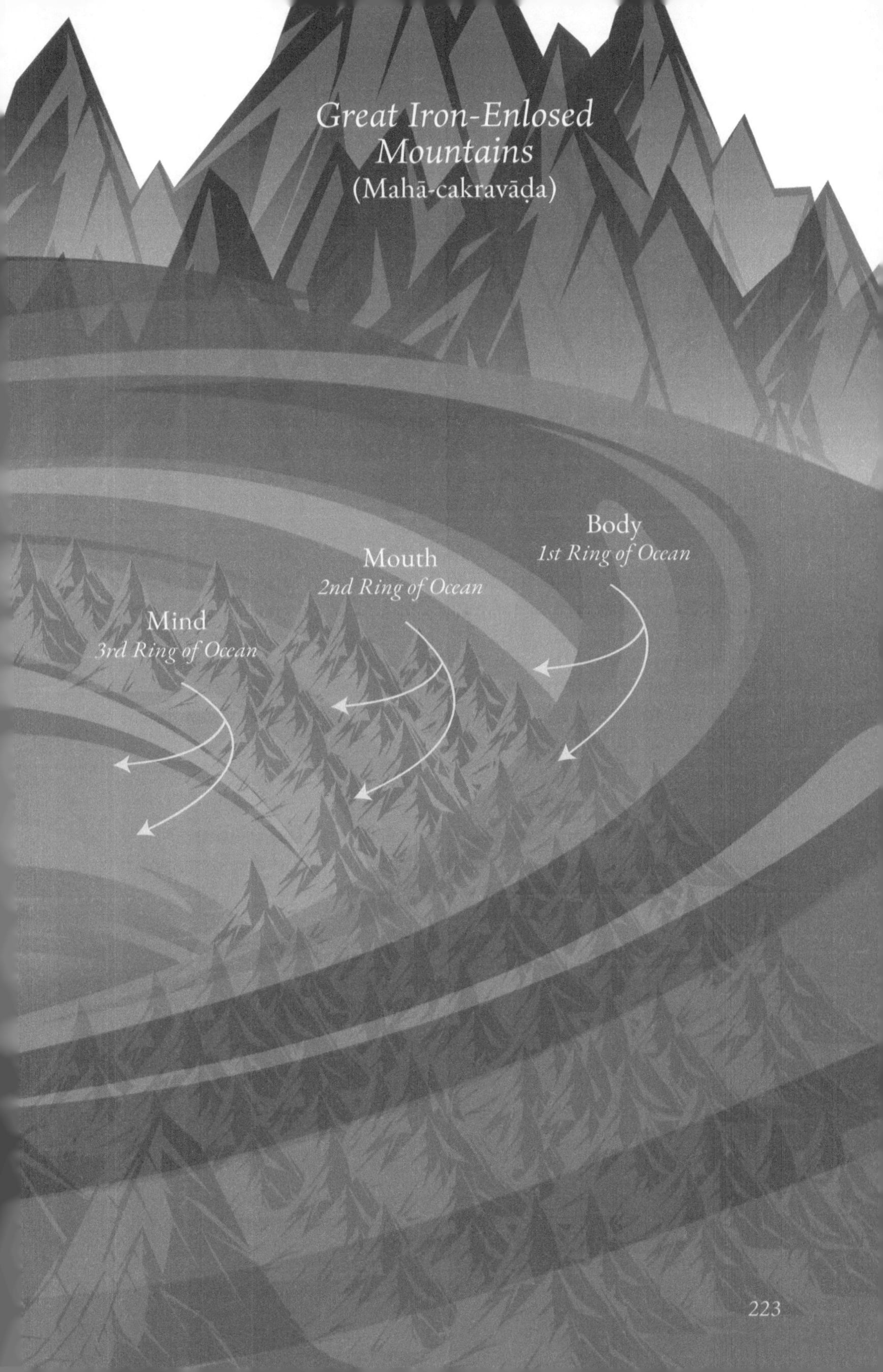

Great Iron-Enlosed Mountains
(Mahā-cakravāḍa)
Body
1st Ring of Ocean
Mouth
2nd Ring of Ocean
Mind
3rd Ring of Ocean

Sanskrit - A Simple Guide

• Each letter or set of letters represents *one* Sanskrit sound with each syllable pronounced. Whereas in English, for example, letter "a" can be pronounced *apple* or *ate*, and syllables are sometimes silent, such as the "a" in *temperature*. A few exceptions (*tv, sv, jñ*) are listed in Compound Consonants.

• The lines and dots are called "diacritics" or "diacritical marks", used because the Sanskrit alphabet has more letters than the English alphabet. Thus, diacritics are combined with Roman letters to represent new sounds.

• For vowels with a dash above them such as *ā, ī* and *ū*— Elongate the pronunciation to about twice as long as their non-elongated counterparts *a, i* and *u*.

• Sanskrit is spoken "flat", but a soft accent can be placed on the third-to-last syllable such as "*samantavipula*" or "*icchantika*". However, this rule does not apply to compound words such as *kṣiti-garbha* and *bodhi-sattva*.

Sanskrit spelling in this sūtra follows IAST, the International Alphabet of Sanskrit Transliteration. You may find the same word spelled differently in other transliteration systems:

<u>IAST</u>		<u>Other spellings</u>	
c	avīci	*ch*	avī*ch*i
ch	*ch*andas	*chh*	*chh*andas
kṣ	*kṣ*itigarbha	*ksh*	*ksh*itigarbha
ś/ṣ	*ś*ākyamuni / tuṣita	*sh*	*sh*akyamuni / tu*sh*ita
ṛ	dṛdha-pṛthivī	*ri*	d*ri*dha-p*ri*thivi

Our gratitude to the following for their resources (can be found online): *Introduction to Sanskrit* by Thomas Egenes, *A Practical Sanskrit Introductory* by Charles Wikner and Sanskrit guides by FPMT and Yoga International.

The following is a guide of English pronunciations that sound similar, but not necessarily equivalent, to the Sanskrit letters.

Vowels

a	p*u*p / b*u*t	ā	f*a*ther / p*a*lm
i	s*i*t / h*ea*t	ī	s*ee*k / m*ee*t
u	p*u*t / s*ui*t	ū	t*oo*l / b*oo*t
ṛ	*r*id / *ri*ver	ḷ	jewe*lr*y (between *l* and *r*)
e	g*a*te / *eigh*t	ai	*ai*sle / p*ie*
o	h*oe* / p*o*le	au	h*ow* (between *owe* and *awe*)

ṃ   s*u*m / *o*m (sa*ṃ*gha becomes nasal sound *ṅ*—sa*ṅ*gha)

ḥ   (slightly aspirated or echo of preceding vowel)

Semi-Vowels

y	*y*ard	r	*r*ed	l	*l*aw	v	*v*ase

Sibilants

ś	*sh*ine	ṣ	effi*c*ient	s	*s*un

Consonants

k	*k*id	kh	bun*kh*ouse	g	*g*o	gh	*gh*astly	ṅ	ki*ng*
c	*ch*at	ch	chur*ch*ill*	j	*j*oy	jh	*j*oy*	ñ	e*n*joy
ṭ	*t*omato	ṭh	an*th*ill*	ḍ	*d*art	ḍh	re*dh*ead*	ṇ	u*n*der
t	wa*t*er	th	*Th*ailand*	d	*d*ough	dh	a*dh*ere*	n	ge*n*tle
p	*p*in	ph	u*ph*ill	b	*b*ut	bh	a*bh*or	m	*m*other

using more breath

Compound Consonants

kṣ	a*ct*ually
tv / sv	also *tw* or *sw*—sat*tv*a, sat*tw*a / *sv*aha, *sw*aha
jñ	also *gy* or *gñ*—pra*jñ*ā, pra*gy*ā, pra*gñ*ā / *jñ*āna, *gy*āna, *gñ*āna

Chanting during Illness and Pain

Nama ārya-Kṣitigarbhāya Bodhisattvāya Mahāsattvāya*
Rid my guilt and sin!

Nama ārya-Kṣitigarbhāya Bodhisattvāya Mahāsattvāya
Enlighten me!

Nama ārya-Kṣitigarbhāya Bodhisattvāya Mahāsattvāya
Transform my body!

Nama ārya-Kṣitigarbhāya Bodhisattvāya Mahāsattvāya
Save my life!

Nama ārya-Kṣitigarbhāya Bodhisattvāya Mahāsattvāya
Cure my illness!

Nama ārya-Kṣitigarbhāya Bodhisattvāya Mahāsattvāya
Heal my wound!

Nama ārya-Kṣitigarbhāya Bodhisattvāya Mahāsattvāya
End my pain!

Nama ārya-Kṣitigarbhāya Bodhisattvāya Mahāsattvāya
Take away my suffering!

Nama ārya-Kṣitigarbhāya Bodhisattvāya Mahāsattvāya
Remove my fear!

Chant each line 4 times before chanting the next.

Composed by the late
Master Sheng Chang Hwang

**ārya* is a Sanskrit word meaning "noble", "excellent" or "venerable".

*Nama ārya-Kṣitigarbhāya Bodhisattvāya
Mahāsattvāya*

Master Hwang's Frequent Sayings

Kṣitigarbha (Earth Treasury) Bodhisattva is most distinguished
among all Bodhisattvas for His Grand Vows—
Kṣitigarbha vows that He would not become a Buddha
until all sentient beings in the six realms,
including those in hell, are rescued and guided onto the
path to become Buddhas.

This Sūtra reminds us that being born as a human is a rare
occurrence. The chance to know Kṣitigarbha's name,
see His image and learn about His merits is the
most precious gift of our lifetime.
Not only will our destinies be altered for this lifetime,
but the destinies of our infinite future births and deaths will also
be altered for the best.

The Buddhas and Bodhisattvas are most lenient, kind and
merciful—they only rescue and give blessings,
never lay guilt nor punish.

All our sufferings and misfortunes come from our defying
and going against the Buddha's teachings.
If we accept and uphold the Buddha's teachings in our lives,
we will depart from the Eight Sufferings—
birth and living, aging, ailing, dying, parting with the loved,
meeting with the hated, having wishes unfulfilled and
experiencing constant agitation.

The Sutra of Ksitigarbha's Fundamental Vows

9 798218 126889